A Piece of Mirror
and Other Essays

First Edition, 2004
Reprinted 2005, 2006, 2007

Copyright Soka Gakkai © 2004

A Piece of Mirror and Other Essays
by Daisaku Ikeda

Published by Soka Gakkai Malaysia (SGM)
Wisma Kebudayaan SGM
243, Jalan Bukit Bintang, 55100 Kuala Lumpur, Malaysia
Tel: 603-2141 2003

Art Design: Chew Meng Tatt

Printed in Malaysia by Napoleon Printing
No.21, Jalan 10/108C, Taman Sungai Besi, 57100 Kuala Lumpur, Malaysia

ISBN 983-41522-3-X

Publisher's introduction

A *Piece of Mirror and Other Essays* covers twenty-three essays written by the President of Soka Gakkai International, Daisaku Ikeda. In these essays, Mr Ikeda expounded his thoughts on various issues that we face. The issues that he wrote on include "Recipe for a happy marriage", "Raising children", "A sense of purpose", "Dealing with stress" and "Thoughts of peace".

In his essays, Mr Ikeda frequently stresses on the humanistic approach of care and concern in our dealing with the varied problems that we face. In applying this approach, he mentioned the importance of personal contact and face-to-face dialogue.

Mr Ikeda in his essays also gives us practical advice as to how we should face issues such as, marriage, how to raise our children, fatherhood, how to overcome stress, coping with the loss of people we loved, and the fear of death.

These essays were published in The Philippines weekly magazine, *Mirror Weekly* in 1998 and 1999.

Soka Gakkai Malaysia was given the permission to publish these essays in a book. We do hope that the readers would benefit from the thoughts of Mr Ikeda and be encouraged by the words he wrote in his essays.

Soka Gakkai Malaysia

Contents

A piece of mirror

A reflection on war and motherhood

I have a mirror. I always keep it with me. Actually, it is nothing more than a piece of broken glass about the size of my palm. A piece of broken mirror, somewhat on the thick side, the kind you could probably find on any trash heap.

But to me, it is anything but trash. When my mother married, she brought as part of her trousseau a mirror stand fitted with a very nice mirror. How many times it must have clearly reflected her face as a young bride! Twenty years later however, the mirror somehow got broken. My eldest brother, Kiichi, and I sorted over the fragments and picked out two of the larger ones to keep.

Not long after that the war broke out. My four elder brothers went off one by one to the front, some to fight in China, others in South-east Asia. I felt very strong feelings of revulsion against the war effort. My four brothers, who were in the prime of life, ready to work and contribute to our family, were taken from us, each by a single piece of paper — the conscription notice.

I will never forget the disgust and anger with which Kiichi, on leave from China, described the inhuman atrocities he had seen committed there by the Japanese army. Japan was wrong, he said, and he felt deeply for Chinese people. I developed a profound hatred for war, its cruelty, stupidity and waste.

Tragically, the Pacific War saw the savage rampage of Japanese nationalism across Asia. The Japanese became emissaries of hell, causing

"The piece of broken mirror speaks to me about those hard-to-describe days of my youth, my mother's prayers, and the sad fate of my eldest brother." *(Room of Mother, Haneda Peace Centre, Ota Ward, Tokyo.)*

untold suffering and grief to both our Asian neighbours and the citizens of Japan. We must never forget the terrible cruelties we inflicted on the beautiful countries of Asia. I offer my sincere apologies for the untold misery caused by the Japanese military at that time.

My mother, her four oldest sons taken away from her, tried not to show her grief, but she seemed to age suddenly. Then the air raids on Tokyo began and soon they were a daily occurrence. I kept my piece of mirror always with me, sticking it carefully inside my shirt as I dodged my way through the firebombs that fell all around us.

The war had cast its shadow into every single corner of our lives. Finally, the end that we all knew was coming arrived. Defeat. On August 15, the war, which had been started and fought in the Emperor's name, now ended with the Emperor's voice on the radio, urging the Japanese people to "... bear the unbearable." At seventeen, my heart was torn between hope and anxiety.

People just sat around in a daze. But then we realised that the skies were quiet for the first time in months. A sense of relief seemed to spread. That night we could turn on the lights at last. How bright! I thought — what a good thing peace is. We were all relieved, but no one dared come right out and say, "I'm glad we lost. Thank goodness the war's over."

My mother's only wish, her only hope, was for the safe return of her sons. She was particularly worried about Kiichi. We had not heard a word from him since he reported having left China for South-east Asia. From time to time, my mother would tell us that she had seen Kiichi in a dream, and that he had told her he would soon return.

Eventually, nearly two years after the war ended and after my other brothers had returned, one by one, we received notification that Kiichi had been killed in Burma. I thought at once of the piece of mirror I knew he carried in the breast pocket of his uniform. I could imagine him, during a lull in the fighting, taking it out and looking at his unshaven face in it, thinking longingly of his mother at home.

When my mother received the news of Kiichi's death, she turned her back to us, shuddering with grief. This was the greatest loss, the deepest sadness she experienced in her life. I felt, in the depths of my being, the tragedy and waste of war. War, which brings such suffering to a mother who is guilty of no crime whatsoever, is an absolute evil.

War brings only suffering and misery to ordinary people, to families and mothers. It is always nameless and unknown people who suffer and moan amidst the mud and flames. In war, human life is used as a means to an end, an expendable commodity. It is said that it takes 20 years of peace to make a man, but only 20 seconds to destroy him. This is why we must always oppose war — neither engaging in it ourselves nor permitting others to do so. All rivalries and conflicts must be resolved, not through power, but with wisdom and through dialogue.

In the dark and troubled times after Japan's defeat, I left home and moved into lodgings. The room was small, bare and ugly, but fortunately, I had my piece of broken mirror with me. Every morning before I went to work I would take it out and use it while I shaved and combed my hair.

In 1952, when I married, my wife brought along with her a brand-new mirror stand, and from then on I looked at my face in the new mirror. One day, I found my wife with the piece of old mirror in her hand and a puzzled look on her face. When I saw that the mirror was likely to end up in the trash basket if I did not speak up, I told my wife about the history attached to it. Somewhere she managed to find a neat little box of specially beautiful wood and she stored the piece of mirror away in it. The mirror is still safe in its box today.

The piece of broken mirror, whenever I look at it, seems to speak to me about those hard to describe days of my youth, about my mother's prayers and the sad fate of my eldest brother, and it will continue to do so as long as I live.

Recipe for a happy marriage

"The two most important ingredients are a sense of gratitude and a common goal."

How a husband and wife should be with each other is not a simple matter. Sometimes circumstances conspire in a strange way, so that wealth or an easy life can actually drive a couple apart, whereas what looks like a mountain of problems to an outsider can be the time of greatest happiness that draws the two closer together.

Unlike the kind of trust that wavers depending on the situation, true love, in the deepest sense of a bond between two people, is something that develops in the face of rough seas. But this does not mean that one partner has to always give in to the other, or that the happiness of one can be built on the suffering of the other.

The husband is not the centre of the relationship, nor is the wife. It is not a question of who is the leader or who must make himself or herself a sacrifice for the other's success and happiness. Just like a song is a marriage of music and lyrics, husband and wife are equal individuals who, at the same time, perform a single melody of life together. What is important, I think, is how beautiful a song these two life partners can create together.

In order to achieve a deep and harmonious relationship, I believe the two most important ingredients are a sense of gratitude and a common goal.

"Just like a song is a marriage of music and lyrics, husband and wife are equal individuals who, at the same time, perform a single melody of life together." *(A photograph of SGI President Daisaku Ikeda and his wife, Kaneko.)*

In today's society, perhaps a family could be thought of as an aeroplane. Buffeted by the winds of change, the two co-pilots have the responsibility of assuring safe arrival. The stability of an aeroplane in flight requires clear direction, momentum and constant effort. And a successful flight requires that the co-pilots keep the same destination in sight.

I heard a story about a woman who felt depressed for a long time and eventually spent her days in bed. A doctor who knew her and her husband well wrote a prescription and gave it to her husband. When the woman saw the prescription she was shocked. It said, "When your husband gives you this medicine, please make sure to take it only after you have said 'thank you' clearly to him three times." She thought this was strange, but since it was underlined, she did say "thank you," three times before taking the medicine. She then realised that she had not used those words for a long time. Every time she repeated "thank you," three times, her health and happiness came back bit by bit. A humble expression of gratitude makes a person beautiful not only in heart, but also in appearance. (Needless to say, this lesson applies equally to husbands!)

One English proverb says: "Keep your eyes wide open before marriage and half shut afterwards." Both husband and wife must try to be tolerant, and have a big heart which forgives minor faults and mistakes by the other. If you are being constantly scrutinised and criticised, you will not feel like trying to change, even if you know that what has been pointed out is true.

I would like to share another story that says a lot about the love between husband and wife. This is from the *Gift of the Magi* by O. Henry. It is about a young married couple called Della and Jim who were poor and lived a barely-furnished rented apartment. It was the day before Christmas and they had both been working out what to give each other to show their love. The wife, Della, wanted to give her husband a watch chain to go with the gold watch he inherited from his grandfather, which he was very proud of. She found that it costs $21 and all she had was $1.87. She decided that the only thing to do was to sell her beautiful brown hair, which was so long that it reached to her knees. In whatever country or culture, a woman's hair means almost as much as life itself to her. But Della made the sacrifice, selling the hair to a wig-maker, and she bought a platinum watch chain with the money.

Her heart pounding with excitement, she waited for her husband to come home. He returned at last, and when he saw her, he was dumbfounded. The present he had brought for her was a pair of beautiful tortoiseshell combs to wear in her long hair. Della assured him that her hair will grow long again in no time and held out her hand with the platinum watch chain gleaming in it. Jim collapsed on the couch, then said with a smile, "Dell, let's put our Christmas presents away and keep them a while. They're too nice to use just now. I sold the watch to get the money to buy your combs."

This story, with humour and pathos, demonstrates through the gifts they gave each other, just how deep was the love between them. Each had sacrificed something very dear to buy a suitable present. But when they presented their gifts, they discovered that there was no longer a gold watch to attach the chain to, and no longer any beautiful brown hair to wear the tortoiseshell combs in. Both gifts had turned out to be useless to them. A practical-minded young couple of today might point out that if the husband and wife had only discussed before what they were going to give each other, they could have saved themselves the waste. But the story deals with something that far transcends that kind of calculating logic. It concerns the beauty of the deep love between husband and wife.

Love takes a thousand different forms. Sometimes the husband may appear to be impossibly domineering to outsiders; yet a couple manages to get along with a surprising degree of harmony. On the other hand, there are cases where the wife seems to have her way in everything, but still an atmosphere of peace prevails. It is not, in fact, the outward appearance that matters. I always think that when a couple has shared the joys and sorrows of life over a long period of time, a deep tie develops between them that cannot be severed by outside forces. This is not the kind of open, direct love we might see amongst young couples. It is something broad and deep, a sense of shared destiny.

I have known some twenty or thirty older couples who seem to possess this power, and I have felt the atmosphere of indescribable fullness and maturity it creates. You will find among such couples none of the tedious, whining talk of some old people. And, although many of them have not lived easy lives, there is no gloom in their expressions. You will find only the sense of deep self-sufficiency that comes when two people have successfully made their way over life's rough places together, along with an appreciation of the preciousness of their remaining time together.

Young love

**"If you sacrifice your own growth and talent for love,
you absolutely will not find happiness."**

It is as natural for young people to fall in love as it is for flowers to bloom in spring.

And yet, the agonies of love are many and varied.

While everyone is free to fall in love or be attracted to someone, and no one has the right to meddle in your private affairs, I feel it is also important not to lose sight of pursuing your own personal development. There are of course no rules on love and marriage, and no one has the right to restrict you in any way. But I hate to see young people getting involved in frivolous relationships, and suffering and agonising over them when they should be fulfilled and happy.

My mentor in life, Mr Toda, often said that when women act with dignity in relationships, problems can be avoided. Women, he said, should not have an easy-going, careless attitude concerning love, as this may lead to regrets and suffering.

While I am writing this with young women particularly in mind, much of what I am saying also applies to young men.

To me, love should be a force that helps us expand our lives and bring out our potential with fresh vitality. This is the ideal, but all too often, people lose all objectivity when they fall in love.

The question is "Does this person inspire you to work harder, or distract you from what you have to do? Does their presence make you

"If you find that you are neglecting things you should be doing, forgetting your purpose in life because of the relationship you are in, then I would guess that you might be on the wrong path. A healthy relationship, in my view, is one in which two people encourage each other to reach their respective goals, while sharing each other's hopes and dreams."

more determined to devote great energies to your activities, to be a better person? Do they inspire you to realise your future goals and work towards them? Or is that person your central focus, overshadowing everything else?"

If you find that you are neglecting things you should be doing, forgetting your purpose in life because of the relationship you are in, then I would guess that you might be on the wrong path. A healthy relationship, in my view, is one in which two people encourage each other to reach their respective goals, while sharing each other's hopes and dreams. A relationship should be a source of inspiration, invigoration and hope.

Rather than becoming so love-struck that you create a world in which only the two of you exist, it is much healthier to learn from those aspects of your loved one that you respect and admire, and continue to make efforts to improve and develop yourself. Antoine de Saint-Exupery, the author of *The Little Prince*, once wrote, "Love is not two people gazing at each other, but two people looking ahead together in the same direction."

Of course, much of daily life tends to be ordinary and unexciting. Making steady efforts to improve ourselves can be trying. And then, when you fall in love, life seems filled with drama and excitement and you feel like the leading character in a book. But if you lose yourself in love just because you are bored, and veer from your path in life, then love is nothing more than escapism. But sadly many people believe that this kind of love is the be-all and end-all, deluding themselves that as long as they are in love, nothing else matters.

Even if you try to use love as an escape, the euphoria is unlikely to last for long. If anything, you may only find yourself with more problems along with a great deal of pain and sadness. However much you may try, you can never run away from yourself. If you remain weak inside, suffering will only follow you wherever you go. You will never find happiness if you do not change yourself from within. Happiness is not something that anyone else, even a lover, can give you. You have to achieve it by yourself. And, the only way to do so is by developing your own character and capacity as a human being, by fully maximising your potential. If you sacrifice your own growth and talent for love, you absolutely will not find happiness.

My concern in saying this is purely for the sake of young people — particularly young women who are often very vulnerable to persuasion by young men. They can sometimes act as if they are stunned and lose their ability to make calm, rational decisions. Since young women are the ones who most often get hurt, they have every right to assert their dignity and look after their own welfare.

It is precisely for this reason that I feel it is important for young women to develop inner strength and self-respect.

It is demeaning to be constantly seeking approval. If you find yourself in a relationship where you are not treated the way your heart tells you you should be, I hope you will have the courage and dignity to decide that you are better off running the risk of being alone for the time being rather than enduring an unhappy relationship.

Real love is not two people clinging to each other; it can only be fostered between two strong people secure in their individuality. A shallow person will only have shallow relationships. If you want to experience real love, it is important first to develop a strong self-identity. True love is not about doing whatever the other person wants you to do, or pretending that you are something you are not. Ideal love is fostered only between two sincere, mature and independent people.

My Wife, Kaneko

"What is necessary in a marriage are very ordinary things like care and consideration."

My wife, Kaneko, is a woman who fills me with admiration. She is a partner and a companion, at times a nurse and an invaluable assistant, at times like a mother, a friend or sister. But most of all she has been my best and closest comrade through all life's struggles.

I was once asked by a women's magazine what award I would give her for her efforts since she married me. This was a very difficult question! In the end I said I would give her a 'Smile Award'. The magazine people also asked me to express a few words of appreciation to my wife. So I said, "My marriage has been the greatest and most precious happiness in my life. I would tell my wife that if I was to be born again, I would hope to be married to her again and again, in lifetime after lifetime, throughout eternity."

My wife knows the truth about me better than anyone, and I think I know her devotion and patience better than anyone else could. So, I would ask her if she could be there for me always. But maybe this sounds more like a help wanted advertisement, than a message of thanks!

Generally speaking, Japanese men are rather clumsy when it comes to expressing appreciation, or words of affection to their wives. I hope men in other countries are much better in this respect. Quiet mutual understanding can be fine at times, but if these emotions are expressed verbally, I am sure that the relationship between a husband and wife will

SGI President Ikeda says: "I have a very busy life and Kaneko helps by keeping a record of everything that happens to me ... My wife often worries about my health and my tendency to overwork."

become much richer and more fulfilling. When one speaks frankly and openly, from the heart, about the things that matter most, one freely reveals oneself, making it possible to be better understood and loved by others.

Marriage begins, after all, with two strangers thrown together. If you forget this very simple fact, you start to expect more and more from your partner, and this can lead to dissatisfaction and eventually to friction in your relationship. The bond that brings a married couple together must be forged so it is even deeper than the ties between blood relations. And such a bond can only be based on the depth of one's character.

I think what is necessary in a marriage are very ordinary things like care and consideration. Just like the sun, rising from the east every day, something ordinary and constant is always necessary in life. There is no instant magical formula to a good marriage. I think our relationship is in some ways built on very ordinary foundations.

I have a very busy life and Kaneko helps by keeping a record of everything that happens to me. She used to say to me: "Such and such a thing happened exactly a year ago," or "It was just like this two years ago." Initially, I was very impressed by her good memory. Then I realised the secret was the five-year diary she kept!

I call my wife "Lieutenant," because she is always giving me advice and cautioning me about various matters. Women tend to be more practical than men, and view everything with the strength of a realism rooted in daily life. No man can match a woman's keen intuition to see through to the essence of things, her depth of wisdom and her ability to take calm action.

My wife often worries about my health and my tendency to overwork. When I was young and we were first married, I suffered from TB and I was not expected to live beyond 30. It has been wonderful for me to have her watching attentively over me all these years, and seeing her smile often made me feel better than any medicine.

Kaneko is never without a smile. And she is so optimistic that she often amazes me. She says, "I've learnt a lot, having gone through many hardships with you. And I've come to the point where I am never taken by surprise now, no matter what happens."

When we married, my mentor Mr Toda gave her the following advice: Whatever unpleasant things may fill your day, always send him — me, that is — off and greet him back home with a smile. This may seem like a very simple advice, but I think that it has taken great reserves of strength and wisdom to put into practice every day, as Kaneko has done. I cannot describe in words what a positive influence her smile has had on me, particularly at times when I was exhausted or stressed from work. She says that while most people consider a smile the result of happiness, she sees a smile as the cause of happiness.

Her success in following Mr Toda's words comes from her deep understanding of life. If she was not so very strong, I do not think she would have been able to maintain her constant optimism. Her motto is: "You may not always win, but never give in to defeat, whatever the circumstances." Her constant encouragement and care have enabled me to overcome great obstacles. In fact, I feel that our history is really the history of my wife's daily victories.

Our life together has not been easy. I have been devoting myself to a struggle to create a new age in which human life and happiness are valued above all. It has not been an ordinary life, and every day has been turbulent and eventful. At times I have been the subject of unfounded slanders and criticisms, and I was once jailed on trumped-up charges. I have always been surrounded by people and there are many demands on my attention and time. Yet, somehow, the more hardships we faced, the more we could strengthen our bond as comrades, as human beings, and as a couple. Everyday the bond between us gets deeper and deeper. And I know it will continue to deepen forever.

I have tried to write poems about my wife, and to take photographs of her, but often when we look at each other, we start to laugh, or she starts to scold me. However, I will end by sharing a poem I gave my wife some years ago:

Opening a new path
Together with you,
My inseparable companion and support.

My mother

"From the plain, unassuming way she lived, I learnt many important things about life."

My mother was an ordinary Japanese woman like many other women born in the late 19th century. She devoted herself to her somewhat difficult husband, and raised eight children, seven boys and one girl. I was the fifth son. There were also two adopted children, making a total of ten. Her life was by no means an easy one. My father, who died in 1956, was so hard-headed and obstinate that he was known among his relatives and neighbours as "Old Diehard." I know my mother must have needed enormous patience to stick with him until the end of his life.

Mother also helped with the family seaweed business. Producing seaweed takes a fearful amount of time and hard work. During the harvest season, she went out every day in a small boat during the early hours of the morning, dipping her hands into the freezing salt water to reach the seaweed — her hands were always sore and chapped. On top of that she had the cooking to do and the children to look after. Still, she always kept the house clean, dusting throughout, sweeping and finishing by carefully wiping each *tatami* (rush) mat with a cloth. She often carried a baby on her back as she washed clothes by hand, or patched up our clothes late into the night.

I never saw her take a break or a nap once. I assume that she was too busy to even stop and think about what she lived for. But she excelled as a homemaker. She could not possibly have done the huge amount of housework she did and keep us fed and neatly dressed if she had not

SGI President Ikeda giving his mother a piggyback as they spent some time together. Mr Ikeda could recall the days how his mother often carried him on her back as she washed clothes by hand, or patched up the clothes late into the night.

been well-organised and methodical. She was so efficient it was almost artistic. There was no movement wasted, and nothing was put in a certain place without meaning and purpose. She was not exceptional in any way, but I consider my mother to have been a great woman.

Life was hard for women in those days. Men dominated society, allowing women few opportunities and choices. However, my mother drew on her inner strength and endlessly gave for the sake of her family in an extremely tough environment. She used to call us "the champions of poverty," and she always stayed cheerful, never complaining. Whatever I was going through, her presence gave me great hope and courage.

My mother's words are permanently engraved on my heart. At times they seem to shine like the light from a diamond. I can still feel her warm and caring voice within me — it heals me mentally and physically. It encourages me to do the right thing and helps me determine what is right or wrong. The words that I remember most are not extraordinary. "Don't do anything that causes others trouble," and "Don't tell lies." When we began school she added, "Once you decide to do something, take responsibility for it and carry it out yourself."

I also learnt from her actions. In spite of the large number of children she had to cope with, in everything, from the dividing up of food to the settling of quarrels, she showed fairness and impartiality. She was in fact a highly skilled judge and arbitrator.

I remember one time when we were cutting up a watermelon and sharing it. One child, who had finished his portion, said to my mother: "I know you don't like watermelon. Can I have your share?" To which my mother replied: "Oh, I've suddenly come to like watermelon," and set aside a slice for another child who happened to be absent. I have a very vivid memory of my mother's voice and expression at that time. It has remained with me to this day and I remember being moved by her even-handed love. Even as an adult, she never forgot how important such small things are to a child.

One incident that showed me her great inner strength took place during the war. In March 1944, as the bombing of Tokyo intensified, we were ordered to evacuate the house in which I had grown up. The house had to be torn down to make a fire break. Just as we had managed to move all the family belongings into my aunt's house and were ready to move ourselves, an air raid targeted her neighbourhood. Flames shot up all around us. My aunt's home took a direct hit and burnt to the ground. The only thing my younger brother and I managed to pull from the flames was an old trunk. In the hazy light of the next morning, we opened this trunk, our sole remaining possession.

Inside was a single umbrella and some of the large decorative dolls usually displayed in Japan on the day of the Girls Festival, March 3. Of all the useless things to survive the flames! We moaned in disappointment. Even though she must have shared our deep frustration, my mother refused to give in to it. "I'm sure that we will come to live in the kind of home where we can display these dolls properly. I'm certain of it...." Her words provoked a smile, then laughter. In that laughter we found hope.

Another wartime incident is engraved in my memory: I remember watching an American B-29 being shot down by anti-aircraft fire. I stood transfixed, as the young pilot parachuted to the ground. I later heard that he was attacked by some people in the crowd that had gathered, before being dragged away by the military police. When I told my mother about this, she replied with genuine feeling, "How terrible. His mother must be so very worried about him." It was irrelevant to her whether the pilot was an enemy or not. Her response impressed me greatly.

My mother was a very ordinary person who seemed content to live a quiet life in her own small corner of the world. And yet, from the plain, unassuming way that she had lived, I learnt many important things about life. From her example, I strongly feel that there is no reason for a mother to feel at a disadvantage or think badly of herself just because she doesn't have a high level of education. A woman who tries to learn from everything and has the confidence to fully use the wisdom she gains in her daily life will give an irreplaceable example to her children.

My mother was able to say to me, just a week before she died "I have won in life." How many people can say that with confidence?

Mother and child

"The influence of a mother on her child is like the
air around him, invisible, but supreme in its
power and importance. Even without words, a mother's
outlook on life will naturally be communicated
to her child and influence him."

The mothers of this world deserve the greatest respect because they have the greatest power and responsibility — that of bringing forth and nurturing new life. The well-being of each family, every society or nation, even the entire world, ultimately lies on their shoulders. I wish to congratulate all mothers struggling to raise children — your precious work is actually creating the greatest possible value. I hope you take great pride in what you are doing.

The influence of a mother on her child is like the air around him, invisible, but supreme in its power and importance. Even without words, a mother's outlook on life will naturally be communicated to her child and influence him. Through contact with their mothers, children can learn how to bear up under difficult circumstances. They also develop the ability to tell right from wrong and the courage to stand up for what is right.

Children watch everything their mother does. If a child sees her mother telling a lie, and thinking nothing of it, that becomes her first lesson in how to be a skilful liar. On the other hand, if their mother is always forward-looking and lively, though they may never win material

"When the sun is obscured, so is the whole world. But when the sun smiles, the whole world sighs with relief. A mother is truly like the sun, warming everyone, often suffering on behalf of others and even regarding doing so as a joy."

wealth or social status, children will inherit the most valuable of all treasures — a spiritual strength that can never be broken. Such inner fortitude is what determines whether a child will lead a life of happiness or unhappiness.

And generally speaking, the more difficult her family's circumstances become, the stronger a mother is. If the mother is strong, her family will be invincible, regardless of the hardships they face.

In *The Grapes of Wrath*, John Steinbeck's famous novel about a family who travel westward across the United States in search of work during the Great Depression of the 1930s, the author describes the indestructible strength of "Ma," the mother of the family. Father asks of the move to the west, "Can we, Ma?" She replies firmly, "It ain't 'can we?' — it's 'will we?' As far as 'can', we can't do nothin', not go to California or nothin'; but as far as 'will', why we'll do what we will."

The land of their dreams turns out to be overcrowded with families desperate for jobs, and the family suffers a series of tragedies. Steinbeck describes Ma's refusal to give up as follows: "Her hazel eyes seemed to have experienced all possible tragedy and to have mounted pain and suffering like steps into a high calm and a superhuman understanding." She let her soul shine through, like the sun high above dark clouds of suffering. "And since old Tom and the children could not know hurt or fear unless she acknowledged hurt and fear, she practised denying them in herself." So she conquered herself first, never being impatient or complaining.

When the sun is obscured, so is the whole world. But when the sun smiles, the whole world sighs with relief. A mother is truly like the sun, warming everyone, often suffering on behalf of others and even regarding doing so as a joy.

However, I do not feel it is always right to praise the showering of a mother's selfless, sometimes overpowering love on a child. Some mothers, because of their strong, blind love, indulge their children's wishes too much and in the end spoil them. What was originally meant for the child's happiness may actually make him miserable later on, as he will struggle to adjust once he interacts with other people, realising that he is not the centre of the world. Sometimes gentleness needs to be paired with discipline if a mother is to teach her child how to be truly human.

An ancient Chinese tale describes how the mother of a powerful General scolded her son who had come home in triumph from battle. She refused to let him into her home. Through a messenger she scolded him, saying, "What have you done? Your soldiers were poorly fed while you were eating luxurious dinners. You sent people to die in battle while you sat in comfort in the General's chair. You may have won the battle, but your leadership was false. You are not my son. I will not let you enter my house." Fortunately he listened to his mother's powerful words and developed into a stronger and wiser leader who cared for his people.

No matter how busy a woman is with work, household chores and parenting, it is also important never to neglect one's own growth as a human being. Children are looking for examples in parents, people they can respect and look up to. Hence, a mother's own inner development is a lifelong process that should not be forgotten. Effective mothers are not mothers who gain satisfaction from having sacrificed their lives for their children. Effective mothers are those who continue to polish and improve themselves.

A woman who has lost awareness of herself as an individual and has no desire to grow may be thanked for all she's done, but her ability to inspire respect from her children will be limited. A mother's way of living — her character — is the most precious treasure she can give her children.

Almost every mother has loving arms and a brave heart, but what counts is how broad her outlook is. Only a woman who has a love of justice and a desire for peace will have the courage and confidence to treat everyone with affection, and be able to raise children with a strong spirit, creativity and broad-mindedness.

And when women extend their motherly love, not only to their own children but also to the whole of society, and they unite with other mothers to speak out against the wrongs in society, I believe they will start to change our world.

I would like to share some lines from a poem of mine, called 'Salute to Mothers'.

Salute to Mothers

Mother
you are sublime,
noble, indomitable.

You are gentle
yet stronger than anyone.
Always smiling,
you can be engaging or
intimidating.

And while you
may appear child-like
you are a perceptive student of life
with a doctoral degree
in daily living.

Through suffering, joy or sadness,
you always create a realm
of ease and comfort.

You are a brilliant physician
healing the heart's wounds.

Your own heart
is deeper than the ocean,
with your open, truth-seeing eyes,
your warm, familiar smile.

Forging bonds of joy
with everyone you meet,
you engage in the compassionate
fight for human rights, for peace,
always advancing
one further step towards a better world.
No one can match or better you —
not the famous
not the politically powerful.

Completely unconcerned
by your lack of wealth,
you smile, serene and unperturbed.

You prepare your simple fare,
laughing, praising yourself,
"Better than the best restaurant!"
You celebrate cramped housing as
"More efficient and easier to clean!'

When people slander, you know
who is a liar
who is a hypocrite
who is driven by jealousy.
Your powers of perception

are unrivalled by
any prosecuting attorney.

Never submitting
to the power of authority
or malicious lies,
you are a mother
of truth and justice.

To you, my gratitude.
To you, my most
profound respect.

Raising children

*"In order for a child to develop an independent self,
it may be necessary at times to discipline him,
while at other times the child needs to follow his own way."*

I love to see the growth of young people, as they are straight and true, and full of promise. Their whole lives lie ahead of them. And it is they who are entrusted with the future. That's why I take them very seriously. For the sake of humanity in the twenty-first century, I want to help today's children expand the inner kingdoms of their hearts as much as possible.

I feel that 'treasures of the heart' is the greatest possible gift from parents to their children. Some parents may wish to guarantee their children's happiness by giving them material wealth. Yet, no matter how wealthy they are, without good health and physical strength, children will not be able to lead truly happy lives. And above all, I believe that it is the 'treasures of the heart' — inner qualities such as spiritual strength, character and humanity — that will ensure the true happiness of a child.

I see child-raising as a process of leading a young adult to develop the strength to stand and walk on his own feet. Every time I meet a child, I always offer my respect to him or her as an independent person. A child is an individual with a distinct personality, and even the bond between parent and child is ultimately a relationship between two individuals.

Some children are very considerate and always deep in thought. Others may be looking for someone to fight with. One child cannot resist scribbling on everything in sight. Another is always running to the kitchen

SGI President Ikeda says: "Every time I meet a child, I always offer my respect to him or her as an independent person. A child is an individual with a distinct personality, and even the bond between parent and child is ultimately a relationship between two individuals."

for something to eat. There are a thousand different character types and each has different interests. Parents can try to anticipate the different directions in which a child's individuality might lead them and then do everything possible to provide the environment best suited for their development.

Children are very sensitive; I always feel it is unkind to make comparisons among them. Buddhism teaches that just as cherry blossoms are cherry blossoms, and plum blossoms are plum blossoms, each person has a totally unique character. Children need to each grow at their own rate and in a way that is true to themselves.

Nothing encourages the growth of children more than knowing they are understood and trusted by their parents, as a story about the great French writer and poet Victor Hugo illustrates. The man who lived next door to the young Hugo's family had a huge apple tree, and he decided to build a fence around it so that children could not pick the apples. Hugo's mother told him, "If you're building that fence to keep my son away, you needn't bother." The man continued to watch, but the boy never came near the tree. I am impressed that Hugo's mother knew her son's character so well.

In order for a child to develop an independent self, it may be necessary at times to discipline him, while at other times the child needs to follow his own way. In my view, strictness is best applied in early years, and as a child grows older he or she should be left more and more to exercise independent judgment on how to behave.

In Japan, the opposite course is all too often adopted. When small, the child is consistently spoiled, and then later a sudden and frantic effort is made to control him. By that time it is too late. A child will never develop a true sense of self-reliance in this way.

I do not think children are weak and fragile from the beginning. I believe that even a newborn baby possesses vast untapped potential. I have heard that a baby, even without any swimming lessons, can instinctively swim when put in water. Perhaps it is the parents' over-protectiveness that actually suppresses the potential of a child, making him or her feeble to the point where the child loses the once-possessed skill and strength needed to swim in the vast ocean called 'life'.

Fearing their child may become wet from a small wave, some parents would make sure that she will not even go near the water, and others may try to shield and protect her by getting wet themselves. Imagine how shocked and helpless such a child may become when suddenly thrown into the vast ocean. What will happen to her after she grows up and is swept away by the crushing waves of life and finds that no one is there to intervene on her behalf?

Parenting to me means helping a child to develop his or her own strength to strive, to challenge and to live. "If you love your child, help him stand on his own feet and send him off on a journey of learning," was a concept popular in old Japan. This is how parents back then educated their children. If the ability to face life's difficulties is made the focus of their upbringing, there is no need to worry whether or not one's children will handle their lives well.

Sadly, however, some parents try to use their children as a means to give expression to their own vanity and pride, trying to force them into some preconceived mould they consider desirable. This is not a pretty sight, and they run a grave risk of destroying the individuality of their child entirely. If a parent thinks not of the child's dreams but of his or her own, the result will be something as artificial as the dwarfed trees in a *bonsai* arrangement.

It is crucial that parents understand the way the children's minds work. When he asks the all-important question, "Why?" and is scolded, or a nonsensical answer is made up to quiet him, a child's purity of spirit will be sullied. One of the most crucial aspects of child-raising is how to answer this frequent question. In the beginning children expect their parents to teach them about everything. However, rather than responding immediately, maybe the mother or father can take the time to work out together with the child what the answer might be. This can help cultivate the child's power of reasoning.

The positive influence of skilful parents is shown in the life of Thomas Edison, who invented the light bulb, the phonograph, and many hundreds of other items we now use every day.

As a child, Tom was curious about everything. Before he had fully grasped scientific principles, he wanted to create a human balloon. He asked one of his friends to drink a liquid mixture of tartaric acid and bicarbonate of soda, thinking that his body would fill up with gas and he would float off like a balloon! Instead, of course, his friend got sick and Tom's usually patient parents scolded him severely for testing his experiments on a human being. Edison later said it was his parents' disappointment at that time that made him decide to invent only things that would be genuinely useful to humanity.

When she was sure he had learnt his lesson, Tom's mother bought him a science book so he could learn how to create experiments safely. She did not just scold him and leave it at that; she could see beyond his mistake to where his talent lay, and she warmly encouraged the development of that talent. Later, after only three months at school, he was dismissed for being a slow learner, but his mother taught him every day at home and soon people were calling him a genius. His brilliant inventiveness was nurtured by his parents' deep love.

If parents can raise their children in a way that discourages self-absorption and fosters open-mindedness, such openness of spirit will naturally develop into a warm-heartedness directed towards others, towards nature and towards the universe. And with such young people in it, I am confident that the world will become a better place.

What is happiness?

"You will never find happiness if you don't challenge your weaknesses and change yourself from within."

What is the purpose of life? It is to become happy. Whatever country or society people live in, they all have the same deep desire: to become happy.

Yet, there are few ideals as difficult to grasp as that of happiness. In our daily life we constantly experience happiness and unhappiness, but we are still quite ignorant as to what happiness really is.

A young friend of mine once spent a long time trying to work out what happiness was, particularly happiness for women. When she first thought about happiness, she saw it as a matter of becoming financially secure or getting married. (The view in Japanese society then was that happiness for a woman was only to be found in marriage.) But looking at friends who were married, she realised that marriage did not necessarily guarantee happiness. She saw couples who had been passionately in love suffering from discord soon after their wedding. She saw women who had married men with money or status but who fought constantly with their husbands.

Gradually, she realised that the secret of happiness lay in building a strong inner self that no trial or hardship could ruin. She saw that happiness for anyone — man or woman — does not come simply from having a formal education, from wealth or from marriage. It begins with having the strength to confront and conquer one's own weakness. Only then does it become possible to lead a truly happy life and enjoy a successful marriage.

She finally told me, "Now I can say with confidence that happiness doesn't exist in the past or in the future. It only exists within our state of life right now, here in the present, as we face the challenges of daily life."

I agree entirely. You yourself know best whether you are feeling joy or struggling with suffering. These things are not known to other people. Even a man who has great wealth, social recognition and many awards may still be shadowed by indescribable suffering deep in his heart. On the other hand, an elderly woman who is not fortunate financially, leading a simple life alone, may feel the sun of joy and happiness rising in her heart each day.

Happiness is not a life without problems, but rather the strength to overcome the problems that come our way. There is no such thing as a problem-free life; difficulties are unavoidable. But how we experience and react to our problems depends on us.

Buddhism teaches that we are each responsible for our own happiness or unhappiness. Our vitality — the amount of energy or 'lifeforce' we have — is in fact the single most important factor in determining whether or not we are happy.

True happiness is to be found within, in the state of our hearts. It does not exist on the far side of some distant mountains. It is within you, yourself. However much you try, you can never run away from yourself. And if you are weak, suffering will follow you wherever you go. You will never find happiness if you do not challenge your weaknesses and change yourself from within. Happiness is to be found in the dynamism and energy of your own life as you struggle to overcome one obstacle after another. This is why I believe that a person who is active and free from fear is truly happy.

The challenges we face in life can be compared to a tall mountain, rising before a mountain climber. For someone who has not trained properly, whose muscles and reflexes are weak and slow, every inch of the climb will be filled with terror and pain. The exact same climb, however, will be a thrilling journey for someone who is prepared, whose arms and legs have been strengthened by constant training. With each step forward and up, beautiful new views will come into sight.

My teacher used to talk about two kinds of happiness — 'relative' and 'absolute' happiness. Relative happiness is happiness that depends on things outside ourselves: friends and family, surroundings, the size of our home or family income. This is what we feel when a desire is fulfilled, or something we have longed for is obtained. While the happiness such things bring us is certainly real, the fact is that none of this lasts forever. Things change. People change. This kind of happiness shatters easily when external conditions alter.

Relative happiness is also based on comparison with others. We may feel this kind of happiness at having a newer or bigger home than the neighbours. But that feeling turns to misery the moment they start making new additions to theirs!

Absolute happiness, on the other hand, is something we must find within. It means establishing a state of life in which we are never defeated by trials, and where just being alive is a source of great joy. This persists no matter what we might be lacking, or what might happen around us. A deep sense of joy is something which can only exist in the innermost reaches of our life, and which cannot be destroyed by any external forces. It is eternal and inexhaustible.

This kind of satisfaction is to be found in consistent and repeated effort, so that we can say, "Today, again, I did my very best. Today, again, I have no regrets. Today, again, I won." The accumulated result of such efforts is a life of great victory.

What we should compare is not ourselves against others. We should compare who we are today against who we were yesterday, who we are today against who we will be tomorrow. While this may seem simple and obvious, true happiness is found in a life of constant advancement. And, the same worries that could have made us miserable can actually be a

SGI President Ikeda greeting Natalia Satz (1903-1993) upon her arrival for a visit to Tokyo. Madam Natalia Satz, who is regarded as the mother of the children's arts movement in Russia and beloved by children all around the world, met with President Ikeda seven times.

source of growth when we approach them with courage and wisdom.

One friend whose dramatic life proved this was Natalia Satz, who founded the first children's theatre in Moscow. In the 1930s, she and her husband were marked by Soviet Union's secret police. Even though they were guilty of no crime, her husband was arrested and executed and she was sent to a prison camp in the frozen depths of Siberia. After she recovered from the initial shock, she started looking at her situation, not with despair, but for opportunity.

She realised that many of her fellow prisoners had special skills and talents. She began organising a 'university', encouraging the prisoners to share their knowledge. "You. You are a scientist. Teach us about science.

You are an artist. Talk to us about art." In this way, the boredom and terror of the prison camp were transformed into the joy of learning and teaching. Eventually, she even made use of her own unique talents to organise a theatre group.

She survived the five-year prison sentence, and dedicated the rest of her long life to creating children's theatre. When we met for the first time in Moscow in 1981, she was already in her 80s. She was as radiant and buoyant as a young girl. Her smile was the smile of someone who has triumphed over the hardships of life. Hers is the kind of spirit I had in mind when I wrote the following poem on 'Happiness':

A person with a vast heart is happy.
Such a person lives each day with a broad and embracing spirit.
A person with a strong will is happy.
Such a person can confidently enjoy life, never defeated by suffering.
A person with a profound spirit is happy.
Such a person can savour life's depths while creating meaning and value
that will last for eternity.
A person with a pure mind is happy.
Such a person is always surrounded by refreshing breezes of joy.

A sense of purpose

"We realise our purpose in life by doing our very best
where we are right at this moment, by thinking about
what we can do to improve the lives of
those right around us."

"Why was I born into this world?" is a question which everyone asks themselves at least once in their life. I believe that having a deep sense of purpose — knowing in the depths of one's being what one was born for, is a great source of happiness.

A successful entrepreneur once remarked that even among the world's wealthiest people, those who lack a real sense of purpose in life often spend their final years in lonely solitude. Sometimes, having amassed great wealth and realised all their worldly ambitions, he found that they were left with a sense of emptiness and meaninglessness.

On the other hand, to be filled each day with a rewarding sense of exhilaration and purpose, a sense of tasks accomplished and deep fulfilment — people who feel this way are happy. Those who have this sense of satisfaction, even if they are extremely busy, are much happier than those who enjoy great ease and leisure but feel empty inside.

A clear sense of purpose gives birth to courage and wisdom. It enables you to look beyond the victory or defeat of the moment and see things in their true perspective. It can fill each instant of life with joy, even in the midst of trying circumstances.

Whatever their occupation — mother, company employee, artist,

"To create value and contribute to the world, what do you need? You need to develop and polish your character until it shines. Small, steady efforts to develop yourself are what will lead you to the greatest happiness in the end. By making consistent effort, the direction you should take will open up before you quite naturally, just as wide, new horizons open up before someone walking up a hill."

fisherman or farmer, I believe that each person has their own path in life; a unique mission that only they can fulfil.

Discovering this purpose or mission is a lifelong task. It is not something that someone can tell you or that comes upon you all of a sudden. You, yourself, must find the reasons for living, the unique contribution that is yours and yours alone to make.

Buddhism uses the example of flowering fruit trees — cherry, plum, pear, etc — to illustrate how each person has a unique mission in life. A cherry tree fulfils its purpose by blooming and bearing fruit as a cherry tree. It never tries to be anything other than itself. It never imitates the blossoms of other flowering trees or wastes time being jealous of them. Rather, it patiently bears the frosts and snows of winter, drawing energy from the earth itself, pushing its roots deeper into the soil. Then, with the arrival of spring, in a burst it unleashes all the life force that it had been storing up, sending forth countless blossoms.

Everyone has some kind of gift. Being talented does not mean just being a good musician, writer or athlete. There are many kinds of talent. You may be a great conversationalist, or make friends easily, or be able to put others at ease. Or you may have a gift for telling jokes, selling things or living economically. You may be punctual, patient, reliable, kind or optimistic. Or you may love taking on new challenges, be strongly committed to helping others, or have an ability to bring them joy. Without doubt, you possess your special jewel, your own unique talent.

In the same way, each of us has a mission that only we can fulfil. That mission will not be found somewhere far away, in doing something special or extraordinary. Even those people who seem to have led great lives have really only done what they felt they had to do in order to truly be themselves.

We realise our purpose in life by doing our very best where we are right at this moment, by thinking about what we can do to improve the lives of those right around us.

I often think of the life of Rosa Parks, an ordinary African American woman returning home after a hard day's work in the tailoring section of a department store by bus one evening in December 1955. Although the bus driver ordered her to give up her seat to a white passenger, as the discriminatory laws of the times required, she refused. Her single word, "No." — the courage of this one ordinary woman — changed history, and her ordinary day took on an eternal significance. Rosa Parks was arrested for her resistance and this set off an explosion of righteous anger among the African American population, largely because of the regard in which she was held — she was respected in her community as a cheerful, warm and intelligent woman. A boycott of the bus service was organised, and within a year segregated busing had been declared illegal throughout the United States.

When I first met Rosa Parks I was struck by her warm personality. She was humble and yet I could see that she was a person of unbending conviction. Now in her eighties, Rosa Parks remains an untiring champion of civil rights, working especially to share hope and a vision of the future with the young people she loves so dearly. Through her sense of conviction, this solitary individual became a leader who transformed the world. One moment of bravery opened the path of her mission in life.

You cannot discover and realise your purpose in life with half-hearted efforts. To follow the dream in your heart and fulfil your mission requires true courage. Not the courage of battlefield heroes, but a courage much closer to home. Most of us, before being defeated by a problem, are first defeated by ourselves. A weak-spirited or cowardly person, before hesitating at the wall of an obstacle, will shrink before his own shadow, frightened by his own imagination, and will be ultimately undone by the coward in his own heart.

Courageous people are first masters of their own heart. I firmly believe that courage is the key that opens the door to happiness.

To create value and contribute to the world, what do you need? You need to develop and polish your character until it shines. The ultimate strengths in life are not a clever tongue or wealth; nor fame or power. The real 'weapon' or 'tool' for living a successful life is what is left over when all empty artifice has been stripped away — the quality of your character as an individual. And small, steady efforts to develop yourself are what will lead you to the greatest happiness in the end.

You will not find your mission by standing still. The way to find it is by challenging yourself in something — I would almost say it does not matter what. Then by making consistent effort, the direction you should take will open up before you quite naturally, just as wide, new horizons open up before someone walking up a hill. Little by little you will come to understand your mission. That is why it is so important to have the courage to ask yourself what it is that you should really be doing now, at this very moment.

It is likewise important to set your sights high. The greater the tasks you choose to take on — one step at a time — the more rewarding and joyful your life will be. If you decide to dedicate your life to a truly noble objective, such as the work of creating a peaceful world for future generations, then you will be able to savour a truly deep sense of satisfaction and happiness.

A person with a strong sense of mission is a source of light. For such a person, there is no darkness in the world. And just as a single lighthouse can guide many ships through dangerous waters, a single person shining with the light of genuine happiness can help friends and family — their entire society — find the smooth open waters of peace and fulfilment.

On women's beauty

"Women tend to find themselves caught in a trap
that makes them eager to fit themselves in the mould of
'the beautiful woman' — a standard set by the
social trends of the time."

I find a woman's face weathered from numerous storms in life to be beautiful. No matter what her age, just like the beauty of grains on wood that deepens with passage of time, beauty that has endured hardships shines with a distinctive splendour.

When one sees a woman for what she really is, free of decoration or cosmetics, I believe her life in all its naturalness, and her true, indestructible beauty emerges. But what is this elusive quality called beauty?

In ancient Chinese literature the so-called beautiful woman looks thin and fragile. Her feet are tiny, because they have been bound, and she looks frail, almost sickly. That seems to have been the preference at a certain time. But later, in the T'ang dynasty, an ideal woman was someone voluptuous and healthy-looking. Even today, many cultures consider plump women to be beautiful and young women are strongly encouraged to eat well. This may sound incredible to women who live in societies where tall and thin models set the trend for what is considered beautiful.

In my country, Japan, too, the definition of beauty seems to vary according to the times. Beautiful women who were portrayed in wood-block prints during the Edo period had long faces, thin eyes and large, protruding chins. But, after World War II, women who were quite buxom

"A woman's true beauty lies not in her appearance, but deep within her heart. A woman who makes all-out efforts and who exerts herself wholeheartedly in her field is beautiful; she really shines!"

were suddenly considered attractive. This makes me question how there can be such different standards in society concerning women's beauty.

Women tend to find themselves caught in a trap that makes them eager to fit themselves in the mould of 'the beautiful woman' — a standard set by the social trends of the time.

The purpose of this endless pursuit, and to whom it is for, are often forgotten. Perhaps, in the end, the pursuit of beauty is actually for yourself, so that you can feel good when you look at yourself in the mirror. If the purpose of beauty is to be attractive to others, then, I would honestly recommend that this time and energy be spent on polishing and cultivating your inner self; your character, as I think that would be much more effective in serving your purpose.

Whether it be your boyfriend, husband, or friends ... why are they attracted to you? I am sure it is not only because of your looks but because of who you are, what they find in you, the beauty of your mind and your personality. No matter how pretty a woman is, if her attraction is only in her physical looks, I do not think the appeal will last, but rather fade away with time. True, lasting attraction to another human being comes from an inner beauty and confidence that shine from within.

I once heard a story from a woman who had gone to her 20th high school reunion. She made an astonishing discovery. Most of the women who had been beauties in their youth looked rather dull, while many of those who had been plain now shone with an inner beauty. As she talked to these friends from many years back, she realised that some of those who had been beautiful had not had to make much effort to attract attention, and this rather self-satisfied attitude had stayed with them through the years, while the more plain-looking women had clearly been working to develop themselves and had become truly attractive as human beings.

For me a woman's true beauty lies not in her appearance, but deep within her heart. A woman who makes all-out efforts and who exerts herself wholeheartedly in her field is beautiful; she really shines. She looks sharp and focused and full of confidence. This kind of radiance will always outshine for me any external beauty related to what a woman is wearing. In fact those who are aware of their inner beauty do not need to seek borrowed beauty from outside. And, sadly, those who care only for their physical appearance are often spiritually impoverished and trying to conceal that lack with exterior trappings.

We all long for things of beauty — beauty of nature, of appearance, of life, a beautiful family and so on. But these cannot be gained if we are withdrawn and isolated, just looking at ourselves. We must create better relationships with other people and interact with our community and society with an open heart. We must be kind to nature. It is only through this process that we really grow and cultivate our own beauty.

A woman who can praise, appreciate and wholeheartedly respect those around her is more beautiful than another who is constantly criticising others. In the same way, someone who can find joy and excitement of her own in her daily life, or even in nature and the changes of the seasons, has the warmth and brightness that can give a sense of peace and comfort to others. Being an expert in discovering beauty makes one beautiful.

The famous sculptor, Rodin, once said that beauty is not found in one woman but in every woman. And he identified the source that lights up this beauty as the 'flame in one's inner life'. The flame of a pure heart, the flame of compassion, the flame of hope, and the flame of courage. These flames are the source of light that enable women to shine with beauty.

It is said: "A woman's beauty shines with age." I find so much wisdom in these words. People normally connect beauty and youth, and cannot link the word 'beautiful woman' with 'older woman'. A young woman in her teens is indeed beautiful, but there is a different kind of beauty that is found in women in their 30s, 50s, even 70s. When we seek beauty inside a person, we will realise that a truly beautiful woman is a person whose inner beauty continues to deepen and be cultivated with time.

Buddhism teaches that your physical appearance is a reflection of your inner self. Hence, a truly beautiful woman knows who she is and what her strengths are and is happy and confident to be true to herself.

Today, we live in an age where commercialism determines what is 'beautiful', but please remember that you cannot find true beauty in these fashionable trends. Beauty cannot be bought with money either. Many insecure young women tend to become confused by such messages sent out by the mass producers of today's society, but I feel that appreciating and realising your own beauty means establishing a secure and robust inner self that will not be swayed by outer circumstances.

Every woman can be beautiful. It all begins by believing in your own beauty.

Fatherhood

"In my own family, as I was always extremely busy,
my wife, Kaneko, acted as a 'relay station'
between me and my three sons. She would tell them
where I was, what I was doing and why,
and what my feelings were."

When I was in fourth or fifth grade of elementary school, I was playing near a large pond with my friend and I fell in. I could easily have died. I did not have a lot of stamina. But my friend ran quickly to get my father, and when he heard, my father came running. And he lifted me out of the pond. He was so big — to a child, their father always seems so large. I remember the feeling of his arms lifting me, the sense of having been saved from danger. I have never forgotten this. In that moment, I thought — this is what a father is like, this is the kind of father I have to grow up to be. There was nothing out of the ordinary about my father. He was a man of few words, but his love for his children was very deep and sure.

In my own family, as I was always extremely busy, my wife, Kaneko, acted as a 'relay station' between my three sons and I. She would tell them where I was, what I was doing and why, and what my feelings were. She always gave me an update on the telephone as to how they were doing, and I tried to write them frequent postcards, always sending separate cards to each one.

I felt that my role was to teach my children how to live as decent human beings and hoped that they would have the physical and spiritual

"Fathers – who take the highest pride in their own lives, in whatever path in life they have chosen, who face each challenge with confidence and high spirits – such parents leave their children a truly priceless legacy."

strength to carry through with whatever work they might chose. I was only really strict about one thing: that they never tell lies. Other than that I think I was quite liberal and broad-minded.

I have noticed that children can become withdrawn if their father scolds them too often. While they are usually confident of their mother's love, so they can even understand her nagging as an expression of that love, being scolded by their fathers can be truly frightening. This pain and stress can even cause children to become rebellious. In particular, I believe that both parents should be careful never to scold a child at the same time, as this can leave him or her feeling trapped and friendless.

It is also vital that, no matter how busy fathers maybe, they find the time to get together and talk with their children. And in my experience, it is a mistake to think that children will somehow automatically come to know that we love them. We need to make conscious efforts to share our true thoughts and feelings with them in words, in a relaxed and open way.

There are many ways to keep communication flowing, as the example of Indira Gandhi, and her father, Jawaharlal Nehru, India's first prime minister, shows. He was jailed nine times during the Indian struggle for independence, and while he was in prison, Nehru and his only daughter exchanged letters frequently. Once Indira wrote, "I miss you so much. I keep your room closed, for I hate going into it and finding it all empty and unlived-in." In his reply, Nehru wrote, "Shall I tell you how I reacted ... when you were studying in Switzerland and England? I kept the door between your room and mine wide open. Every morning I visited your room and every night I went there to bid it goodnight. I wanted the room to look bright and airy ... as if you had just gone out and might come back at any moment." After receiving this letter, Indira followed his advice and gave her father's room a thorough cleaning. No matter how high the walls of physical separation, the door between the hearts of father and daughter was always open.

The difficulties faced by fathers who have to work to support their family are immeasurable. They must struggle in a changing economy and rack their brains to succeed in their workplace for the sake of their family. But children often have very few opportunities to see their fathers 'in action' at work. The vast majority of children have no idea how much effort they put in. Often all they see is a figure of exhaustion — someone who comes home from work only to lounge around and watch television. Whatever the demands of his career, I believe that a father should stand firm while tolerating whatever life throws at him, so he can still be the mainstay of the family.

I heard a touching story about a schoolgirl who was ashamed that her father was a plasterer, while the fathers of her friends wore suits and ties to work. She told her mother how embarrassed she was, and her mother took her to the construction site where her father worked. There the girl saw her father on a sizzling hot roof, drenched in sweat, but immersed in his job. "Take a good look at your father who's working so hard in this heat," her mother said. Later the daughter asked her father why he did not become an office worker, so he could be working in a place with a roof, instead of sitting on top of one.

The father grinned and said, "Different kinds of work suit different people. Everyone is doing their best to make a living. But no job is as easy as it looks from the outside. I'm really proud of my work. Please don't ever judge people by their appearance."

The girl thought long and hard about this and began to understand the meaning of her father's words. She resolved, "There's no doubt in my mind anymore that my Dad is the greatest in the world. I'm going to be just like him and do whatever I do the best I can."

Fathers — and mothers — who take the highest pride in their own lives, in whatever path in life they have chosen, who face each challenge with confidence and high spirits — such parents leave their children a truly priceless legacy.

Dealing with stress

"Marriage ranks as the seventh most stressful event,
between injury or illness and losing one's job."

We live in a stress-filled age. Human society everywhere is changing rapidly and the pace of change seems to be increasing. Change and uncertainty are always a source of stress. At the same time, society is becoming increasingly competitive — even children feel the need to compete for grades in schools. And as societies change, the human relations that are so important to sustain people are growing weaker.

An American psychologist once rated the most stressful events in life. Highest on the scale was the death of a spouse, followed by divorce, separation and arrest. Even happy incidents can be a source of stress — marriage ranks as the seventh most stressful event, between injury or illness and losing one's job!

Stress also causes illness. Skin disorders, allergies, asthma, ulcers and cancer have all been linked to stress, showing the intimate link between mind and body. Stress is known to lower the body's resistance, making us vulnerable to a variety of afflictions. And sometimes a person's response to stress, such as overeating or drinking, can be as harmful as the stress itself.

Often, positive qualities in a person — such as a sense of responsibility or a desire for perfection — can actually increase the stress that individual will feel. And, those who are too concerned about how other people view them, what they think of them, will end up creating a great deal of needless stress and worry in their lives.

What is vital is to be true to ourselves, not always comparing ourselves with others. Each of us is the star of our own life story and the

"When we are in a stressful situation, it is easy to start feeling sorry for ourselves, imagining that there is no one more unhappy than us. People struggling with deep stress and anxiety often tend to become isolated and brood over their own suffering."

best way to live is to make our own decisions and follow our own convictions. We should each feel free to be ourselves. People who are not good at expressing their true opinions and feelings have been shown to be very vulnerable to stress.

Insecurity and anxiety, rather than the mere fact of being busy, are what destroy physical and mental health. They say that a machine does not break down from continual use, but that it is the constant friction that eventually wears it down. Worrying and stress are the 'friction' of human life.

Some years back I met with Dr Anthony Marsella, professor of psychology at the University of Hawaii. Among the ideas for dealing with stress he proposed were: a well-regulated daily life; thinking in a positive and constructive way; not putting off things that need immediate attention; taking time to pray, meditate or self-reflect; getting proper nutrition, exercise and sleep; and communication with the people around you.

This reminded me of reading about a town in Pennsylvania, USA, called Roseto where there was an unusually low rate of heart disease — commonly linked to stress. Roseto was founded by Italian immigrants and most of the population there were great eaters. Their diet included a lot of fat and meat, and many were smokers, too. Researchers tried to find out why these people stayed healthy.

They discovered that the town was like one big, happy family, bound together by a spirit of mutual concern and deep personal interaction amongst neighbours. There were many chances for people to communicate and enjoy one another's company. But time passed, and the link of each individual to the community weakened. As a result, although the diet stayed the same, the rate of heart disease gradually rose to the US average.

Having a good friend, someone we can talk to about anything, sharing our ups and downs with complete trust and openness, enables us to regain a sense of balance, of being 'all right'. Humour and laughter are also very important ways of relieving stress.

Simple remedies like sleep, good food, a warm bath or light exercise can help, too. The secret is to use our time wisely and find ways to give ourselves a refreshing change of pace. We should all make sure we have time to relax every day, listening to music or walking in nature — whatever suits us — even for ten to fifteen minutes.

When we are in a stressful situation, it is easy to start feeling sorry for ourselves, imagining that there is no one more unhappy than us. People struggling with deep stress and anxiety often tend to become isolated and brood over their own suffering. A doctor told me that one method of treatment is to bring a group of such people together and guide them to put their energy into thinking about and coming to the assistance of each other. Apparently this kind of group therapy is very successful.

Similarly, it is when we manage to break out of our isolation and take action for others that we can tap new sources of hope and vitality from within.

Thus, in an odd way, simply relaxing and doing nothing may not necessarily be the best way to release stress. Sometimes finding a new interest, something you really want to commit yourself to, can be a more effective 'cure' for stress.

Fortunately, life is naturally endowed with the capacity to convert even the negative into something positive. With stress, the question is whether we use it as the wind beneath our wings to soar high into the sky, or whether we allow ourselves to be blown away by it. We each have the capacity to decide this. I firmly believe that, as Buddhism teaches, our life at its deepest level is shaped by our own inner resolve, our state of mind.

An aeroplane cannot fly without the resistance of the air that lifts it. In the same way, if we lack any resistance in our life, having no problems to challenge us, we can lose our focus and sense of direction. It all depends on whether we can put the 'wind' to good use. As long as we are alive, there will be some stress in our life. The important thing is to learn how to handle it and use it as an impetus for growth, to widen our horizons and find greater happiness.

Staying young

"An active interest in others, finding new pastimes and making new friends — such positive attitudes have been shown to slow physical and mental decline."

When I was younger, I thought I had nothing to do with those who were elderly. I think most young people find it hard to believe that they themselves will grow old. The reality is however, that now I am among the 'elderly', and I cannot move with the speed and ease that I once did.

My teacher used to say that the last years of our life are the most important. If those last few years are happy ones, we have had a happy life.

Old age is a time of spiritual fruition and completion. When people are no longer pursuing position or status, money or material possessions, they can look closely at themselves and at the reality of life and death without the distractions of superficial concerns.

When you reach old age, you know in your heart if you have lived a satisfying life or not. No one else can know this or decide it for you. The single greatest challenge we each will face is whether we can honestly say at the end of our days on this Earth that our life has been well spent.

I believe that whether we can live a truly satisfying life to the end depends to a considerable extent on how we view death. Sadly, many older people are anxious and fearful about death. But, as a Buddhist, I find it helpful to compare the cycles of life and death to the daily rhythms of waking and sleeping. Just as we look forward to the rest sleep brings after the efforts and exertions of the day, death can be seen as a welcome

"Even though our bodies may age, if we maintain an active, positive attitude, our hearts and minds will remain 'youthful' as long as we live. There is a great difference between simply living a long life and living a full and rewarding life. What is really important is how much rich texture and colour we can add to our lives during our stay here on Earth – however long that stay may be. Quality is the true value, not quantity."

period of rest and re-energising in preparation for a new round of active life. And just as we enjoy the best sleep after a day in which we have done our very best, a calm and easy death can only follow a life lived to the fullest without any regrets.

It is natural for trees to bear fruit in the harvest season, and in the same way, 'old age' is a period of ripening. It can be the most valuable time in human life, when we have rich experience, deeply polished character, and a pure and gentle heart. The loss of certain capacities with age is nothing to be ashamed of. Rather, I feel the various infirmities of age should even be seen as badges of honour and worn with pride.

There is a saying that goes: "To a fool, old age is a bitter winter; to a wise man it is a golden time." Everything depends on your own attitude, how you approach life. Do you view old age as a period of decline ending in death, or as a time in which one has the opportunity to attain one's goals and bring one's life to a rewarding and satisfying completion? The same period of old age will be dramatically different depending upon your own outlook.

I received a letter a few years ago from a woman in Kyoto who was then 67 years old. Her advice was as follows: "We need to banish any expression of defeat from our minds — statements or thoughts such as, 'I can't do it,' 'I'm too old,' 'There's no point in my trying,' 'I'm past it,' or 'It's too hard.' Instead we should be telling ourselves: 'I won't give up yet,' 'I'm still young,' 'I can still do it,' 'I've still got plenty of energy.' Just by changing the way we speak to ourselves and others we can change our pattern of behaviour in a positive direction."

Research shows that when people make continuous use of their powers of memory and concentration, these abilities need not fade. An active interest in others, finding new pastimes and making new friends — such positive attitudes have been shown to slow physical and mental decline.

Even though our bodies may age, if we maintain an active, positive attitude, our hearts and minds will remain 'youthful' as long as we live.

To quote the poet, Samuel Ullman, "Youth is not a time of life; it is a state of mind; it is not a matter of rosy cheeks, red lips and supple knees; it is a matter of the will, a quality of imagination, a vigour of the emotions; it is the freshness of the deep springs of life."

It is vital to always look to the future, to have plans and aspirations — such an outlook is crucial to making the last years of one's life rewarding and fulfilling.

One woman whose youthful attitude greatly impressed me was the American painter known as 'Grandma Moses'. She had produced around fifteen hundred paintings by her death at the age of one hundred and one. Yet, she had not even started painting until she was seventy-five. She had never studied painting and was an ordinary farmer's wife until then.

She had faced many difficulties in her life. Five of her ten children died young, and she lost her husband when she was sixty-six. She said that though she had experienced real pain and hardship, she refused to be dragged down by suffering and always looked ahead.

Whatever she encountered, Grandma Moses strove to make each day and each moment shine with her smile. After her surviving children left home and her husband died, she refused to give in to loneliness or step back from life. She took up the challenge of painting, and her last years glowed like a beautiful sunset. She wrote, "I look back on my life like a good day's work. It was done and I feel satisfied with it. I was happy and contented. I knew nothing better and made the best out of what life offered. And life is what we make it; always has been, always will be."

There is a great difference between simply living a long life and living a full and rewarding life. What is really important is how much rich texture and colour we can add to our lives during our stay here on Earth — however long that stay may be. Quality is the true value, not quantity.

Jose Abueva
— Refusing to hate

"Devotion to peace goes with determination
to stop repetition of tragedy."

Every life has its pain and suffering. Without undergoing arduous suffering, there can be no greatness in life. There is not a person in history who has accomplished something great without experiencing suffering or living through some kind of crisis. Pain and sorrow cultivate the vast earth of one's inner being, and enable one to bring forth the desire to work for the happiness of others.

Someone whose life demonstrates this truth for me is Dr Jose Abueva, former President of the University of the Philippines.

Fifty years ago, the sixteen-year-old Jose was rowing a boat in search of his parents who had been taken prisoner by the Japanese armed forces occupying the Philippines. His father, Teodoro Abueva, had refused to cooperate with the invaders of his homeland, and became a member of the anti-Japanese resistance government. Jose's mother, Nena Veloso Abueva, was the head of the Women's Auxiliary Service in the resistance.

The Japanese military had been hunting Teodoro for a long time.

After hiding in the mountains for a year with the guerrilla forces, the Abueva family — except for Jose and his brother, Billy, — had been captured. The Japanese military separated husband and wife and tortured them. The children were forced to listen to their parents' agonising screams. Then the soldiers took Teodoro and Nena away, setting the

Dr Jose Abueva sees youth and cultural exchanges as vital currents in the great flowing river of peace that he is determined to create. *(Manila, The Philippines, May 1993.)*

children free. Billy looked after his brothers and sisters while Jose, together with a cousin, set out in a boat in search of his parents.

It was to be a sad journey. They landed at the town where Jose's parents had been taken. News of the American recapture of the Philippines was spreading, and there was not a Japanese soldier to be seen. Praying that by some miracle his parents might still be alive, Jose searched for a clue to their whereabouts. He heard rumours of people who had been killed and hurled down a cliff, and was advised to start his search there.

He climbed the hill. The sun shone down fiercely from a cloudless sky. He walked into a clearing with some bushes beyond it. Suddenly, an acrid smell hit his nostrils as he came upon an executioner's handiwork. He saw a soiled white shirt with blue stripes and immediately recognised it as his father's. Then he saw a piece of his mother's brown dress. He also found fragments of rosaries and belts that he recognised as having belonged to them.

Despite the horror of the experience, Jose did not cry. He was so emotionally and physically drained, tears would not come. He looked to the shining sea stretching towards Mindanao. Thoughts of what had happened to his parents flooded his mind. They were martyrs who had fought for their love of freedom and their love for their country. For that they had been tortured and killed, and this was the hill where their lives had ended in such a cruel sacrifice

Jose gathered his parents' remains and got back in the boat. The sea of his homeland was almost blindingly beautiful.

Dr Abueva wrote, "Although this happened half a century ago, it is indelibly etched in my mind. I will never be able to forget." How many others like him will have to suffer the cruelty, insanity and demonic nature of war ... memories that will never disappear?

But Dr Abueva showed no trace of bitterness. He once said on a visit to Tokyo: "My parents were killed by Japanese soldiers. But none of us seven children bears any hatred towards Japan. I like the Japanese. And, I believe the people of Japan and the Philippines share the same love of peace."

I was amazed when I heard this: even through his extreme suffering, he has maintained his noble beliefs. Truly he is a great-hearted person. What a contrast he presents to those who murdered innocent, decent people. Why is it that most Japanese have no respect for their fellow Asians? Why can't they see that their very arrogance has made them objects of scorn? And, violence and exploitation continues today, though now the means are economic.

After the war, the orphaned Abueva children pulled together to take care of each other, growing into fine adults. Jose studied at the University of the Philippines (UP) and then the University of Michigan before eventually becoming a professor at UP.

Dr Abueva has served in posts in Nepal, Thailand, the United States and Japan, and his fond memories of his loving parents have sustained him wherever he has gone. Whatever he has achieved in his life, it started with his climb up that hill on that fateful day. He has been utterly devoted to peace, determined to keep others from experiencing the kind of tragedy that he did.

"The great irony of my life," he remarked, "was my recruitment to serve at the United Nations University in Tokyo." For nearly eight years he lived with his wife and family in the country that had murdered his parents. All that time, he was an ambassador of friendship, with a heart as boundless as the sea.

In 1987, he was elected president of the University of the Philippines. "Throughout history there have been many leaders of war," he declared with great passion, "but there have been few leaders of peace. I am determined to help change this."

Abueva was concerned that UP students should be aware of their duty to society, and lead the way in finding solutions to the country's problems.

As president, he put special emphasis on the creation of a 'House of Peace' for international exchange; perhaps a crystallisation of his youthful vow to work for peace. He believes that building deeper relations between peoples is even more important than focusing on relations between governments. He sees youth and cultural exchanges as vital currents in the great flowing river of peace that he is determined to create.

Dr Abueva invited me to the official opening of the House of Peace in May 1993, saying that he hoped it will be a symbol of friendship between the Philippines and Japan.

I also declared my determination to devote my life, as an individual Japanese citizen, to building bridges of friendship between the peoples of Asia.

Who makes history?

"The real heroes of history are ordinary people."
— *Jules Michelet*

If we look across the vast landscape of human history, the life of one human being may seem rather small and insignificant. Yet, while human beings seem to be swept away by the flow of history, it is also clearly human beings who create history.

I believe that the courageous cry of even a single individual standing up for justice can light the hearts of thousands and change the course of human history. I support the view of French historian Jules Michelet that the real heroes of history are ordinary people. As the recent history of so many countries shows, history is made by the people, not just by generals or those in power.

Michelet introduced the story of Madame Legros, an unknown woman who ran a small tailoring shop in Paris, France, before the Revolution.

One day, Mdm Legros picked up a letter dropped in the street. It was written by a political prisoner being held in the Bastille prison, where people could be arbitrarily held on the order of the king. The letter she found was from a political prisoner who had been locked up for more than thirty years. The letter had been meant for a well-connected person who might be able to secure his release.

On reading the letter, Mdm Legros realised that this complete stranger was innocent and she decided to try to save him. She had no social connections whatsoever. She went from door to door, appealing to the master of each household and requesting their help in freeing the

A bronze statue of Napoleon Bonarparte.

prisoner. However, her actions brought nothing but criticism and she was even accused of being the prisoner's lover. As time passed, she lost her shop, her parents died and she was constantly threatened by the authorities.

But she was not perturbed, nor discouraged or afraid; she just kept pursuing her goal with single-minded devotion. Once someone arranged for her to meet a lady-in-waiting to the royal family. She walked the long distance from Paris to Versailles on a bitterly cold day in spite of being seven months pregnant. Finally, her petition reached the king but he replied that he would never grant this prisoner freedom.

Even then, Mdm Legros would not give up. She resolved from now on that she would trust only in the power of the people. She approached anyone she thought might listen, and gradually caused ripple after ripple of public opinion to rise and spread.

She finally had her moment of victory when, in 1784, unable to refuse any longer, the king finally ordered the prisoner's release. The Bastille, long considered impregnable, opened its doors for the first time because of the appeals for justice of one woman.

History takes us back to events and lives long ago. We meet passionate revolutionaries and cowardly traitors. We come to know people who wanted to lead peaceful lives but suffered greatly. We encounter others who pulled themselves up from the depths of suffering to make the impossible possible.

Naturally, as we watch the drama of history unfolds in our minds, we begin to see life from a broader and more expansive point of view. And when we see where we have come from, where we are, and where we are going, this makes it easier to pick out the road we should take.

The study of history is actually the study of humanity, so in a sense knowing history is knowing oneself. It is like the study of the weather patterns. Though we cannot predict the weather with complete accuracy, we can forecast trends based on statistics, on probability. The human heart is also very unpredictable, but by looking at history we can see the trends and probabilities in human actions. We can then use history as a mirror to guide us in shaping the future.

But the history that is recorded and passed on does not always transmit the whole truth. I believe it is vital in this day and age that, rather than draw hasty conclusions from one aspect of the truth, we try to find out the complete truth about an issue. So much of the conflict and hatred in the world today is caused when we make sweeping judgments on the basis of partial knowledge.

For example, it has been widely taught that Christopher Columbus discovered the Americas. But people were already living there long before he got there. It may have been a discovery from the European perspective, but certainly not from the viewpoint of the indigenous

American people.

Tragically, the 'conquerors' of the so-called New World were so self-centred that they did not even regard those indigenous peoples as human beings, slaughtering them or rounding them up as slave labour.

The view that Columbus 'discovered' America legitimised similar actions on the part of others. Within the single word, discovery, lies a self-righteous view of history, a view that justifies the subjugation of other peoples in one's own interest.

History based on the idea of 'discovery' and 'exploration' also teaches only about Magellan the explorer, not Magellan the invader. It fails to teach of the courageous struggles of local inhabitants to defend their homelands.

Such a colonialist view of history lay behind Japan's cruel invasion of Asia as well. From the Meiji period which began in 1868, we Japanese were intent on catching up with Europe and aimed at becoming the 'Europeans' of Asia. As a result, with devastating impact, we treated our fellow Asians in the same way that the Europeans treated the indigenous peoples of America after the arrival of Columbus.

Whatever shameful acts took place, it is extremely important for the sake of the Japanese people and the world that the whole truth be recorded and passed on. Only then can similar tragic errors be prevented from happening again.

Up to now, history has always been centred around the interests of the powerful, around politics and the state. We must rewrite history so that it is centred instead around ordinary people — such courageous individuals as Mdm Legros — and their lives, so that it reflects the viewpoint of all humanity. As Michelet said, "From the first page to the last, history has had but one hero: the people."

The teacher's art

"I firmly believe that every young person has the power
within him or her to change the world. It is the role
of those who teach to believe in that power,
to encourage and release it."

I remember being set a project for one summer vacation during elementary school. We had to make something at home and bring it with us for the new term. Being clumsy, I could not get anything together and had to return to school embarrassed and empty-handed.

When asked what happened to my project, I stammered out that I had forgotten it at home. To my horror, the teacher told me to go home and bring it back right away. I returned home feeling desperate and miserable. Looking around, I saw a bookshelf my older brother had made. I presented this to the teacher, who praised my work and gave me a good grade for it. But, looking back, I am sure that he knew what the real story was.

From one perspective you might say that this teacher was rewarding me for lying, but that is not my view. Through the warm, large-hearted way he embraced me, he communicated to me a very concrete sense of being believed in — really what I needed at that moment. And, of course, I felt deeply ashamed, and vowed never to let such a thing to happen again.

I believe that education is what remains long after the content of each specific lesson we were taught has been forgotten. The essence of education is character formation, teaching young people how to live in

"Teachers who do not understand and care for their students, merely parroting stereotyped answers, cannot possibly satisfy children's curious and sensitive minds. It must never be forgotten that the most important people in a school are its students. And, it is vital that teachers believe in every child's potential and care about their happiness as human beings."

society and encouraging them to think independently. Study is much more than simply absorbing existing knowledge and techniques, and the ability to memorise and reason is nothing compared to the wisdom, emotional richness and creativity that resides within every human being.

Education that does not teach a sense of values turns people into mere robots filled with data but with no understanding of what it is for. Such soulless, over-competitive schooling makes successful children arrogant, while the less academically bright are left with little self-confidence and a deep fear of failure.

Sadly, education is often used to cultivate people who are useful only to the extent that they fit into various slots in society, and school systems in Japan and many other countries actually prevent children from developing their full potential.

In the race to climb the ladder of scholastic prestige and status, we can easily lose sight of the most important question of all: What is the purpose of learning?

I believe that the genuine goal of education must be the lifelong happiness of those who learn. Education should never be subordinated to the demands of national ego, or of corporations searching for profit-generating employees. Human beings, happiness, must always be the goal and objective.

My own teacher, Josei Toda, often said that the greatest error of modern humanity was that it confused knowledge with wisdom. Knowledge itself is a neutral tool that can be used for good or evil. As history sadly proves, educated monsters can wreak far greater horror than their unschooled brothers. At least, seven of the participants at the Wannsee Conference where the Nazis planned the 'final solution' — extermination — to the 'Jewish problem', had doctoral degrees. It is hard to imagine a greater perversion and debasement of education.

Wisdom, in contrast, always directs us towards happiness. The task of education must be to stimulate and unleash the wisdom that lies dormant in the lives of all young people. This is not a forced process, like pressing something into a preformed mould, but rather drawing out the potential that exists within.

I firmly believe that every young person has the power within him or her to change the world. It is the role of those who teach to believe in that power, to encourage and release it.

The relationship between teacher and pupil can be a vital link through which new horizons are opened up and life develops. To me, the essence of education is this process whereby one person's character inspires another. When teachers become partners in the process of discovery, burning with a passion for truth, the desire to learn will naturally be ignited in their students' hearts. And once children feel that their teachers are genuinely concerned for their individual welfare, they will begin to trust them and open up to them.

It saddens me that now this vital bond between pupil and teacher seems to have been weakened by distrust and misunderstanding. Teachers everywhere struggle with problems of control and discipline, and students resent the fact that they must cram their heads full of knowledge that fails to answer their pressing questions about life, the real world and human relationships.

Teachers who do not understand and care for their students, merely parroting stereotyped answers, cannot possibly satisfy children's curious and sensitive minds. It must never be forgotten that the most important people in a school are its students.

I once heard about a Japanese elementary school teacher who was irritated by a girl in his class who was unable to keep up. He gave up trying to help her after a fellow teacher told him, "Human beings are just like fruit; twenty to thirty per cent is always worthless and there's nothing you can do about it."

Then, one day during a break, he noticed the girl playing with a puzzle, trying to put plastic pieces together so that they fit into a box. Finally she succeeded and yelled, "I got it!," her face sparkling with a delight he had never seen before. The teacher suddenly felt remorse. How dare he gave up on her! Was it not his job to make sure that each child walked out of his classroom with the confidence that they could do anything if they really tried?

He discovered that the girl's parents, both graduates of leading universities, were constantly calling her 'stupid'. The teacher resolved to praise her every day, for every little accomplishment, to wash away the stain of criticism from her heart.

After a year, the girl was transformed. Proceeding at her own pace, she came to experience the joy of learning. The key was her realisation that if she made an effort to achieve something, she could do it.

This story shows how the smallest failure can destroy a child's confidence, and the smallest catalyst can trigger growth. It is vital that teachers believe in every child's potential and care about their happiness as human beings.

Women at work

"Each woman must develop her abilities to the fullest, despite these unfavourable conditions, and her steady efforts will eventually gain her recognition and respect in society."

Some years ago, a woman whose husband had died from cancer told me how she managed to get back on her feet again. She had three sons, and when her husband passed away, she explained, she was at a total loss as to what to do. The shock must have been as if the Earth had suddenly stopped turning. It was her depth of love towards her children that enabled her to continue: "I mustn't let my sons lose hope," she vowed to herself.

Although the family was not that hard-up financially, she began working for a construction company. Continuing to take care of her family, she tackled the challenge of mastering her new job. What she wanted to demonstrate through her work, not just to her sons but to the world, was that the family would not in any way be defeated by tragedy.

Most women, of course, work because they have to. Given the hard economic times around the world, there has been an increase in the number of households where both husband and wife must work outside the home.

We should never forget that work is a natural human activity. While we work, our mind is concentrated, our nerves taut, our will engaged — this activity can actually be our greatest protection from the mental and physical ravages of ageing. We become more energised as we focus the

"Most women, of course, work because they have to. Work is a natural human activity. While we work, our mind is concentrated, our nerves taut, our will engaged – this activity can actually be our greatest protection from the mental and physical ravages of ageing."

inherent dynamism and vibrancy of our lives.

Thinking of work only as a way to make ends meet and supplement the family income is bound to cause inner resentment and unhappiness, and lead one to reach a dead end. I hope each individual, man and woman, can see their work as a means of improving themselves, and a way of making a contribution to the world. Rather than a burden, a job should be regarded as a great opportunity for growth. If a woman is convinced that her work is enhancing society's well-being, I feel confident that she has found true liberation — liberation as a human being. As she realises her own worth and expands her horizons, such a woman can inspire a higher level of development not just in other women but in society at large.

Sadly, few adjustments are made to accommodate the needs of working women. Often the work a woman is given makes her feel she is being discriminated against, being assigned jobs less important than her male colleagues. As long as women are ignorant of this situation, or resigned to it, the negative aspects of our male-dominated world will continue unchanged. I believe that each woman must develop her abilities to the fullest, despite these unfavourable conditions, and her steady efforts will eventually gain her recognition and respect in society. Only then will women be able to change society. And the touch and influence of women is definitely needed in order to transform the cut-and-dried world of men into a more humane one. Even the best computer cannot replace creativity, gentleness, warmth or human kindness.

When I was young, I learnt that the Japanese word for 'work' literally means to give ease and comfort to others. Judging from my experience of meeting many people, those who seem to be happy are, without exception, those who are exerting themselves for the happiness of others. As the Buddhist sutras teach, when you light a lamp for others, your own path will also be lit.

The demands of running a household and raising a family are already enormous. When work outside the family is added to this, every day becomes a titanic struggle against time. After working themselves ragged, many women must rush home to cater to the needs of their children, prepare meals and finish household chores. Given all working women are responsible for, I can hardly believe that they ever really rest, even when asleep. But I do think that when you are busy, your mind and body stay fit, and if you are twice as active as others, you can be twice as fulfilled and satisfied with what you achieve in your life. In contrast, there is sometimes a risk that women who spend all their time at home end up worried about trivial matters and never feel the satisfaction of broadening their horizons.

It may help to liken the life of a working mother to a bicycle, with work and the family as its two wheels: the cyclist must keep the two balanced to move along a path filled with numerous obstacles. She needs to have a firm grasp on the handlebars — in other words, a clear understanding of why she is working. She can only learn to master cycling through trial and error: at times, she will put too much weight on work or too little; she may even lose her balance at times. Yet, she has to keep trying and push ahead.

Small efforts can help maintain this balance. A note to her family telling them when she will be home or what to do is a personal touch worth a thousand words from a working mother. Other hints I have gleaned from talking to many working women are; never to mix work matters with family business, to complete the task at hand within that day whenever possible, to be a good listener, and to set specific goals for your career.

Many working mothers are concerned about the impact of their careers on their kids. But according to surveys, the length of time a mother spends with her offspring is not as important as the depth of the love and heart-to-heart communication between them when they are together. A very important factor is for women to have full confidence in their way of living. Children will naturally come to respect and trust their mother if she still manages to give them loving care despite being very busy. In fact, it seems that the sight of their mother striving to fulfil the needs of both her job and family can foster a very balanced attitude in children.

In this fundamentally male-dominated world, more effort is unfortunately asked of women than of men. Their role is indeed demanding; while men need them for the warmth that they still feel uncomfortable expressing, society needs their magnanimity, wisdom and practicality. If women are able to open up their lives through active involvement in society, I feel the value to themselves and all humanity is immeasurable.

Life and death

"Buddhism views the idea that our lives end
with death as a serious delusion. It sees everything
in the universe, everything that happens,
as part of a vast living web of interconnection."

Death is something no one can escape from. It follows life as surely as night follows day, winter follows autumn or old age follows youth. People make preparations so that they will not suffer when winter comes. They prepare so they will not have to suffer in their old age. Yet, how few people prepare for the even greater certainty of death!

Modern society has turned its gaze away from this most fundamental issue. For most people, death is something to be feared, to be dreaded, or it is seen as just the absence of life — blankness and void. Death has even come to be considered somehow 'unnatural'.

What is death? What becomes of us after we die? We can try to ignore these questions. Many people do. But if we ignore death, I believe that we are condemned to live a shallow existence, to live 'hand to mouth' spiritually. We may assure ourselves that we will somehow deal with death "… when the time comes." Some people keep busily engaged in a constant stream of tasks in order to avoid thinking about the fundamental issues of life and death. But in such a state of mind, the joys we feel will ultimately be fragile, shadowed by the inescapable presence of death. It is my firm belief that facing the issue of death can help bring real stability, peace and depth to our lives.

What, then, is death? Is it just extinction, a lapse into nothingness?

"The vibrant energy we call life that flows throughout the universe has no beginning and no end. Life is a continuous, dynamic process of change. Why then should human life be the one exception? Why should our existence be an arbitrary, one-shot deal, disconnected from the universal rhythms of life?" writes SGI President Ikeda.

Or is it the doorway to new life, a transformation rather than an ending? Is life nothing more than a fleeting phase of activity preceded and followed by stillness and non-existence? Or does it have a deeper continuity, persisting beyond death in some form or other?

Buddhism views the idea that our lives end with death as a serious delusion. It sees everything in the universe, everything that happens, as part of a vast living web of interconnection. The vibrant energy we call life that flows throughout the universe has no beginning and no end. Life is a continuous, dynamic process of change. Why then should human life be the one exception? Why should our existence be an arbitrary, one-shot deal, disconnected from the universal rhythms of life?

We now know that stars and galaxies are born, live out their natural span, and die. What applies to the vast realities of the universe applies equally to the miniature realms of our bodies. From a purely physical perspective, our bodies are composed of the same materials and chemical compounds as the distant galaxies. In this sense, we are quite literally children of the stars.

The human body consists of some 60 trillion individual cells, and life is the vital force that harmonises the infinitely complex functioning of this mind-boggling number of individual cells. Each moment, untold numbers of cells are dying and being replaced by the birth of new cells. At this level, we experience daily the cycles of birth and death.

On a very practical level, death is necessary. If people lived forever, they would eventually start to long for death. Without death, we would face a whole new array of problems — from overpopulation to people having to live forever in aged bodies. Death makes room for renewal and regeneration.

Death should therefore be appreciated, like life, as a blessing. Buddhism views death as a period of rest, like sleep, by which life regains energy and prepares for new cycles of living. Thus there is no reason to fear death, to hate or seek to banish it from our minds.

Death does not discriminate; it strips us of everything. Fame, wealth and power are all useless in the unadorned reality of the final moments of life. When the time comes, we will have only ourselves to rely on. This is a solemn confrontation that we must face armed only with our raw humanity, the actual record of what we have done, how we have chosen to live our lives, asking, "Had I live true to myself? What have I contributed to the world? What are my satisfactions or regrets?"

To die well, one must have lived well. For those who have lived true to their convictions, who have worked to bring happiness to others, death can come as a comforting rest, like the well-earned sleep that follows a day of enjoyable exertion.

I was impressed a few years ago to learn of the attitude of a friend of mine, David Norton, professor of philosophy at the University of Delaware, towards his own approaching death.

When he was only seventeen, the young David had become a 'smoke jumper', a volunteer fire fighter who parachuted into inaccessible areas to cut trees and dig trenches to keep fires from spreading. He did this, he said, in order to learn to face his own fear.

When, in his mid-sixties, he was diagnosed with advanced cancer, he faced death head-on and found that the pain did not defeat him. Nor did he find dying a lonely or solitary experience, according to his wife, Mary. She later told me that he felt he was surrounded by all his friends and said that her husband had faced death without fear, regarding it as "another adventure; the same kind of test as facing a forest fire."

"I guess the first thing about such an adventure," Mary said, "is that it's an opportunity to challenge yourself. It's getting yourself out of situations that are comfortable, where you know what goes, and where you don't have to worry. It's an opportunity to grow. It's a chance to become what you need to be. But it's one that you must face without fear."

An awareness of death enables us to live each day — each moment — filled with appreciation for the unique opportunity we have to create something of our time on Earth. I believe that in order to enjoy true happiness, we should live each moment as if it were our last. Today will never return. We may speak of the past or of the future, but the only reality we have is that of this present instant. And confronting the reality of death actually enables us to bring unlimited creativity, courage and joy into each instant of our lives.

Coping with loss

"Buddhism identifies the pain of parting from
one's loved ones is one of life's inevitable sufferings."

The impermanence of life is an inescapable fact. Yet while it is one thing to know, in theory, that each moment of your life may be the last, it is much harder to actually live and act, on a practical level, based on that belief. Most of us tend to imagine that there will always be another chance to meet and talk with our friends or relatives again, so it does not matter if a few things go unsaid.

But whenever I meet someone, I try to extend myself to them to the utmost, for that may be our last encounter. I never leave room for regret, aiming to concentrate my whole being at each moment.

Buddhism identifies the pain of parting from one's loved ones as one of life's inevitable sufferings. It is certainly true that we cannot avoid experiencing the sadness of separation in this life.

Sakyamuni, the Buddha who lived in India over 2,000 years ago, lost his mother when he was just one week old. As he grew up, he always wondered, "Why did my mother die? Where did she go? Where can I go to meet her? What is this thing 'death' that has robbed me of my mother? What, after all, is life?"

His sorrow at the loss of his mother became a powerful driving force which enabled him to have deep compassion for others and to seek the truth of life.

One day he met a woman whose child had died; she was wandering about in a grief-stricken daze with the tiny body clutched to hers. "Please

"Probably no words can heal the heart of a mother who has lost her child. Someone truly wise, on meeting a woman whose child has died, might simply sit down at her side, and stay there not saying a word. Even if no words are exchanged, the warm reverberations of concern from deep in that person's life will be felt."

give me some medicine to save my baby," she begged Sakyamuni, her eyes red with tears.

He knew the child was past saving, but wanted somehow to encourage her. He told her to fetch some poppy seeds so he could make medicine, but only to collect poppy seeds from families which had never known bereavement.

The woman hurried off into town and called on every household. But although many had poppy seeds, there was not a single house in which there had never been a death. The distraught mother gradually came to realise that every family lived with the sadness of lost loved ones quietly concealed somewhere in their hearts. Through this experience she realised she was not alone in her feelings of grief.

Probably no words can heal the heart of a mother who has lost her child. Someone truly wise, on meeting a woman whose child has died, might simply sit down at her side, and stay there not saying a word. Even if no words are exchanged, the warm reverberations of concern from deep in that person's life will be felt.

In the Buddhist view, the bonds that link people are not a matter of this lifetime alone. And because those who have died in a sense live on within us, our happiness is naturally shared with those who have passed away. So, the most important thing is for those of us who are alive at this moment to live with hope and strive to become happy.

By becoming happy ourselves, we can send invisible 'waves' of happiness to those who have passed away. But if we allow ourselves to be overwhelmed by sorrow, the deceased will feel this sorrow too, as we are always together, inseparable.

When I met Sonia Gandhi, widow of Indian Prime Minister Rajiv Gandhi, not long after her husband's tragic death, I said to her, "The lives of those who have suffered the greatest tragedy shine with the greatest brilliance. Please change your destiny into a source of great value. If you are sad, your husband will grieve with you. And if you stand up with a smile, your husband will be happy too." I am happy to say that with great courage and resolve she is now continuing her late husband's work.

A person who meets with a great tragedy will quite naturally be at a loss as to what to do with their life. I believe one has to decide whether to keep up one's spirits and go on living with all one's might or let oneself be broken by disappointment.

There are many examples where people who lost their mother or father early in life have gone on to achieve great things. My friend, Oswald Mbuyiseni Mtshali, a famous South African poet, once told me that the first poem he wrote was to his mother. He said, "My mother's death was a great shock to me, so great that I almost couldn't recover from it. It took me a long time to get over it. But eventually I noticed something. Whatever strength I had was something my mother had given to me, left to me. My mother's words were alive in me; my mother lived on inside me. When I recognised that, a poem to my mother welled up spontaneously from the depths of my heart."

Through struggling to overcome the pain and sadness that accompanies death, we become more aware of the dignity of life and can come to share the sufferings of others as our own.

The Harvard University Library was donated by a woman who had lost her son in the tragic sinking of the *Titanic* in 1912. Her son, Harry Elkins Widener, who died at the age of twenty-seven, was a graduate of Harvard who had a passion for reading and had collected many books. In fact, he had just completed a book-buying trip in London when he boarded the *Titanic* together with his mother and father.

Harry was a loving son to his mother, a gallant and heroic young man. Seeing his mother safely into the lifeboat, he stayed behind with his father on the sinking ship. The collection of over three thousand valuable books that he had already built up was left to Harvard University, but there was nowhere to put them. This prompted his mother to donate huge sums of money so that a library could be constructed. Out of this tragedy came a priceless gift to countless students.

Those who can overcome grief and continue to live with strength and courage deserve respect. I greatly admire someone who can overcome their personal suffering and go on to leave behind something of value for future generations.

Human revolution

"The process of human revolution cannot be undertaken alone. It is through our interactions with others that we polish our lives and grow as human beings."

Life is about expressing and developing our individuality as fully as possible — it is about self-realisation. This process is what I call 'human revolution'.

There are many kinds of revolutions — political, economic, industrial, scientific, artistic, and so on. But no matter how external factors change, the world will never get better as long as people remain selfish and apathetic. As John F. Kennedy said, in 1963, "Our problems are man-made — therefore, they can be solved by man. And man can be as big as he wants."

An inner change for the better in a single person is the essential first turn of the wheel in the process of making the human race stronger and wiser. This 'human revolution' is, I believe, the most fundamental and most vital of all revolutions. This kind of revolution — an inner process of self-reformation — is completely bloodless and peaceful. In it everyone wins and there are no victims.

Life is a struggle with ourselves; it is a tug-of-war between moving forward and slipping backward, between happiness and misery. We are changing constantly, but the real issue is whether we change for the better or the worse, whether or not we succeed in enlarging our narrow, self-centred focus to take a broader view.

"If we succeed in challenging ourselves on a fundamental level, we can change from being a person who is buffeted about by the environment or the people around us, becoming someone who can positively influence our situation and surroundings. We actually create the unique shape of our lives by the infinite choices we make each day."

Every day, we are faced with countless choices and decisions. We have to decide which path to take in order to feel good about ourselves and become better, more generous-spirited individuals. If we just allow ourselves to be ruled by force of habit, the way we have always reacted to a given situation, we will be drawn down the path of least resistance and stop growing as a person.

But if we succeed in challenging ourselves on a fundamental level, we can change from being a person who is buffeted about by the environment or the people around us, becoming someone who can positively influence our situation and surroundings. We actually create the unique shape of our lives by the infinite choices we make each day.

True individuality and character never come to full flower without hard work. I feel it is a mistake to think that who you are right now represents all you are capable of. If you passively decide, "I'm a quiet person, so I'll just go through life being quiet," you will not ever fully realise your unique potential. Without having to change your character completely, you can become a person who, while still basically quiet, will say the right thing at the right time with real conviction. In the same way, a negative tendency towards impatience can be developed into a useful knack for getting things done quickly and efficiently.

But nothing is more immediate, or more difficult, than to confront and transform ourselves. It is always tempting to decide, "That's just the kind of person I am." And unless we challenge this tendency early in life, it will become stronger with age. But the effort is worthwhile in the end, as I believe that nothing produces deeper satisfaction than successfully challenging our own weaknesses. As the Russian author, Tolstoy, wrote, "Supreme happiness is to find that you are a better person at the end of the year than you were at the beginning."

Human revolution is not something extraordinary, or divorced from our daily lives. It often begins in a small way. Take a man who thinks only of himself, his family and friends. Then, one day, he makes a move to break out of these narrow confines just a little, going out of his way to help a suffering neighbour. This is the start of his human revolution.

But this process of human revolution cannot be undertaken alone. It is through our interactions with others that we polish our lives and grow as human beings. In Japan, mountain potatoes known as *taros* are rough and dirty when harvested, but when put in water and rolled against each other, their skin peels away, leaving the potatoes shining and ready for cooking. The only way to hone and polish our character is through our interaction with others.

By taking action for, and being positively engaged with others, we become better and more disciplined people. But this does not mean making others happy while ignoring our selves or our own happiness. The happiness we create as individuals, and the strong bonds we create with each other, result in the happiness of all humankind.

Transforming our own lives at the most fundamental level actually holds the key to changing society. A deep change in our outlook, the inner reality of our life, produces changes in the external workings of our life, in other people, and our community.

I firmly believe that a great human revolution in just a single individual can help achieve a change in the destiny of a nation and enable a change in all humankind.

The life of Mahatma Gandhi illustrates this point. As a boy he was painfully shy. He was always worried people would make fun of him. Even after passing his examinations as a lawyer, he was still timid. When he rose to present the opening arguments in his first court case, his mind went blank from nerves and he had to leave the courtroom.

But a turning point occurred when he was in South Africa, where Indian residents faced severe discrimination. Gandhi was riding in a first-class carriage on a train, when he was ordered to move to the freight car. He refused, and was eventually forced off the train. In the waiting area at the station, Gandhi stayed awake all night, debating whether he should return to India or endure the hardship of taking a stand and fighting for human rights. He finally realised that it would be cowardice to run from his fears and disregard the needs of people who were being discriminated against as he had been.

From that moment, Gandhi squarely faced and challenged his timid nature, determined to challenge injustice. And his inner change sparked one of the greatest developments of the twentieth century — the movement for social change through non-violence.

Every single person has tremendous potential that is largely untapped. Through the hard work of our human revolution, this potential

* 1000% Success of
        Youth Picnic

Fund darkness — Fund enligh
        2 sides of ~~same~~ life
            ~~thing~~

 — Overcome all fund. darkn
 — Appreciation of perfect
        set of circumstances

On Att. Buddhahood.

6-8 Chanting
   am

can be revealed and we can establish an independent, unconquerable sense of self. We can deal creatively with any situation that life has to offer. This open-ended process enables us to keep growing and developing throughout our lives, and beyond. We will never meet a deadlock on our eternal journey of self-realisation.

To my young friends

"Try to be as active as possible. Just by being young you
possess a treasure more valuable than power or fame.
To be young is to have hope, passion and freedom."

Youth is a time of rapid change, from day to day and moment to moment. It can also be a time of confusion. You may feel as if you are standing alone in a wasteland or on a battlefield. Sometimes you may think you cannot believe in anyone, that no one loves you, or even that you have no reason to live.

Grades at school or university are probably not your only worries. You may have problems at home, with money or health, with how you feel about your looks, with members of the opposite sex, or with friends. From feeling confident and upbeat one moment, you may be overwhelmed with insecurity, frustration or apathy the next.

You may have fundamental questions about yourself and your identity: Who am I? What should I do with my life? It is quite natural to feel unsure about the best way to proceed. If you have not yet decided on your future course, I feel the best thing is just to concentrate your energies on what you need to do right now, and gradually your full potential will emerge.

The most important thing is not to give up on yourself when you are young, giving in to negativity or cynicism. Do not compare yourself with others. Be true to who you are and try to cherish and feel content with your own irreplaceable life. Even if you are sometimes laughed at, or people let you down, keep going forward and never let yourself be

SGI President Ikeda meeting some local Nepalese children during his trip to Kathmandu. *(November 1995)*

defeated.

Setting yourself targets is a good idea. Even if you have the tendency to only stick at something for two or three days, just keep renewing your determination. When you are studying and you think, "I can't do any more; I want to go out," you may decide to challenge yourself to keep going for just another five minutes. People who can persevere even this much will achieve great things in life.

Youth is the time for building your foundation in life. You cannot build a tall building without first making its foundations solid and secure. In the same way, if you neglect study or shy away from hard work while you are young, you cannot really build yourself a great future.

A smooth, easy life in which everything goes your way may seem great, but you will not be able to develop your character if everything always works out according to plan. You may even become spoiled — a person who cannot think about others and who is no help when things get tough.

If your parents are poor or lacking education, or they are always quarrelling with each other, try not to think yourself unlucky. This is a truly human situation that will help you develop as a person. You may feel it would have been better to be born into a rich or successful family. But often people who grow up in such a world act like well-behaved automatons, bound by formality, tradition and appearances, lacking genuine warmth and spontaneity.

There is no such thing as a whole life of smooth sailing. Therefore, you do yourself a favour by taking on difficult challenges, forging and strengthening yourself in your youth, while you are healthy and strong. I hope you can see all difficulties as the material that will enable you to develop a big heart and become people of depth and substance.

Try to be as active as possible. Just by being young you possess a treasure more valuable than power or fame. To be young is to have hope, passion and freedom. Your whole life lies ahead of you, brimming with possibilities.

Rather than a life of blank pages, it is better to live a life crammed full of memories of struggles and wonderfully varied experiences. Not to make waves, not to leave behind any history, but just to grow old and die, is a sad way to live.

Do not wait! While still in your youth, you can become the main actors in the human drama unfolding around you, the shapers of history. Even if you feel powerless, that it is difficult to believe in yourself, please try not to be easily swayed by the views of others, and hold true to what you know is right. Try to believe in yourself.

I hope you will develop sharp powers of perception, then lead the way in breaking through the apathy and stagnation of society around you. So many people are complacent, thinking, "Out of all these people, surely someone will do something." Such cowardly people avoid facing problems, assuming that everything will somehow work out in the end.

Please challenge the injustices and corruption you see around you — speak out and fight against any abuses of power and authority that you see. Confront and challenge every situation with the full force of your character. Live with honesty and integrity and produce results. Set your sights high and fight to achieve your goals with your whole being and spirit.

Edward Whymper was a young nineteenth-century English mountaineer who set out to climb the 'unclimbable' — the Matterhorn in the Alps. Since ancient times it had never been scaled. At twenty-one, Whymper determined to succeed where no one had succeeded before. His first attempt failed, but he resolved not to give up, and year after year he pitted himself against the mountain. On one attempt he got within 430 metres of the summit, but he slipped and fell sixty metres and was seriously injured. Another time a rockfall forced him to descend. Seven times he was defeated, but he did not give up. On July 14, 1865, on his eighth attempt, at the age of twenty-five, he finally made it to the top.

Like him, by challenging a great goal, you can break through your limitations and realise incredible growth.

It all comes down to you. I hope you will not rely on others or wait for them to do something. Try to develop such a strong sense of responsibility that you can stand up to the fiercest storms, confidently proclaiming, "I'll do it. Just watch me!" Please confront reality, look it squarely in the face, and with guts, wisdom and strength, challenge everything that lies ahead of you.

The power of words

"Sincere one-to-one conversation can soften and melt even hearts that are completely frozen."

I have vivid memories of encounters with people whose voices or words have moved me over the years. One that springs to mind happened during a visit to the Guilin region of China, a beautiful land of craggy mountains, mists and rivers.

Walking along, we met two young girls, no older than 15 or 16, selling medicinal herbs near a river. They carried a large basket filled with herbs, inviting passers-by to buy their goods with vibrant voices.

"Ni *hao*! [Hello!]" I called to them. "Ni *hao*!" They smiled back. "We offer every kind of medicine: choose the one you want."

I smiled at their high spirits and asked, "Do you have anything to make me smarter?" They seemed taken aback, but only for an instant. "I'm sorry," one of them replied in a clear, firm voice, "We just sold out of that one."

Our group burst into laughter at this witty reply, and we felt as warm inside as if a gentle spring breeze had touched us. As a Chinese saying puts it, "Even a single word uttered out of goodness can warm the heart in the bitterest winter."

I fondly recall that my wife and I ended up buying some herbs as souvenirs, and I sometimes wonder how the girls and their families are doing.

I believe that sincere one-to-one conversation can soften and melt even hearts that are completely frozen. By talking with someone face-to-

"Face-to-face conversation may seem like something very ordinary, but it is in fact the most powerful tool for positive change we possess. We can exchange ideas on a very human, personal level, with a basis of respect and faith in each other's essential goodness. Everyone involved is equal; there is neither superior nor inferior."

face, you can actually change that person's life and your own.

Today, we live in the midst of a flood of soulless information. And, the more we rely on one-way communication, like radio or TV, or static and unmoving words in print, the more I feel the need to stress the value of the sound of the human voice: The simple but precious interaction of voice and voice, person and person; the exchange of life with life.

In a face-to-face conversation, the listener can ask questions or disagree, and this in turn may make the speaker rethink his or her own views. The process is dynamic and multi-faceted, creating mutual joy and understanding.

For myself, I love talking with a wide range of people from all over the world. I always learn something new and I find it inspiring to be exposed to different ways of thinking. This is a kind of spiritual nutrition for me.

My experience is that no matter how strong the initial uncertainty, or even hostility another person may feel towards you, if you approach them with complete sincerity and speak the truth, they will invariably respond in kind.

I remember several years ago suggesting holding a dialogue with representatives of Islam. Some friends tried to convince me this would be very difficult. But I felt we should not let ourselves be held back by such preconceptions. We never know what is possible until we try. I suggested that the dialogue did not need to be a debate over religious doctrine. We could start by talking about the problems that we all face as human beings, focusing on culture and education. Or we could discuss the desire for peace, something shared by people all over the world. I am happy to say that I have since carried out dialogues with several highly-respected representatives of the Islamic world, and SGI members in many countries have also carried out interfaith dialogues with representatives of Islam among other faiths.

Face-to-face conversation may seem like something very ordinary, but it is in fact the most powerful tool for positive change we possess. We can exchange ideas on a very human, personal level, with a basis of respect and faith in each other's essential goodness. Everyone involved is equal; there is neither superior nor inferior.

The French thinker, Montaigne, loved discussion, and he always kept an open mind, saying "no proposition astounds me, no belief offends me, however much opposed it may be to my own. Contradictions of opinion only arouse and exercise my mind." To him, dialogue was the search for truth, and he claimed that he welcomed and embraced the truth, in whoever's hands he found it.

As we have two ears and one mouth, maybe we should listen twice as much as we speak. Certainly if we are self-righteous or prejudiced, no one will approach us with an open heart.

Sometimes our attempts to start a discussion or talk things over may be slighted or ignored. Then we should remember that rejection and disappointment are inevitable in life, and just keep on trying. Maintaining dialogue takes great patience and perseverance. We need to develop a strong sense of self, so that although we can clearly see the emotions of the other person, we keep on calmly and steadily 'rowing' closer to their heart.

The biggest obstacle to successful dialogue is usually excessive attachment to one's own point of view. For instance, a rift between a parent and child will not be easily healed as long as the parent only sees things as a parent and the child only from his or her own viewpoint.

In a genuine discussion, it is best if we can see any confrontations that arise as just another form of our connectedness. If both parent and child can see themselves as sharing common ground — making up a family together — things can take a surprisingly easy turn for the better. The deeper the common feeling that binds us, the more we can embrace those who differ from us and ensure that dialogue will lead to a fruitful outcome.

Whether the problem is that of a single family, or international in scope, if those involved can view things from a higher perspective, with a sense of shared purpose, the gears of dialogue will always start to turn in a positive direction.

If more people were to pursue dialogue in an equally broadminded and persistent manner, I am sure that the inevitable conflicts of human life would find easier resolution. Prejudice would give way to understanding, and war to peace. Genuine dialogue results in the transformation of opposing viewpoints, changing them from wedges that drive people apart into bridges that link them together.

Thoughts on peace

"No matter what justifications maybe offered,
in my view, there is absolutely no such thing
as a just and correct war."

Some people who have seen war stories in the movies or on TV may have been impressed by it; finding it somehow attractive and feeling that the actors looked glamorous and brave.

The reality of war, however, is completely different. It is cruel and filthy, and filled with sadness and misery. Anyone who has actually experienced war knows it must never be repeated. I saw more than enough of the horror of war when I was young, living through air raids in which explosives and incendiary bombs fell like rain. Wandering in a sea of fire; worried out of my mind about my family, feeling terrible sadness and helplessness as I saw people dying around me.

No matter what justifications maybe offered, in my view, there is absolutely no such thing as a just and correct war. War treats human life as a means to an end, and it brings only terrible suffering and unhappiness to ordinary men and women on both sides. Each person who has died in war was irreplaceable and precious — someone's parent, child or friend. That is why we must always oppose war. All conflicts should be resolved, not with violence and brute force, but with wisdom and sustained dialogue.

It may be tempting to think that wars are started by the state, or an alliance of countries. However, in fact, wars are started by the workings of the individual human heart. Buddhism teaches that war is the result of

"Peace can never be attained by passively waiting for it. It is necessary for each of us, no matter how weak we feel we are, to build deep within our hearts a stronghold for peace that can withstand, and in the end silence, the incessant calls to war."

anger and egotism. To overcome the threat of war, we must conquer and subdue the selfish nature that lurks in every human heart.

Natural disasters such as floods or earthquakes cannot be prevented by human reason or wisdom. But problems which are caused by human beings can be resolved by human beings themselves.

Two-time Nobel Prize winner Linus Pauling wrote in his book, No More War: "I believe that there is a greater power in the world than the evil power of military force, or nuclear bombs — there is the power of good, of morality, or humanitarianism. I believe in the power of the human spirit."

I also hold that an inner change in the depths of people's lives can transform egoism and replace it with a loving humanism that seeks peace and coexistence among all people.

So what keeps this 'power of good' from having a greater impact on the world? What hinders progress towards peace? In a single word, it is mistrust. It is the prejudice and preconceptions that grow from mistrust. Often these have roots in past conflicts and rivalries. Without removing this wall of mistrust, and without the effort to discover the goodness that shines in every single human being, no progress towards peace will be possible.

When I first travelled to the Soviet Union in the early 1970s, people wondered why, as the leader of a religious movement, I wanted to visit a communist country that did not recognise religion. I responded, "Because the citizens of the Soviet Union are people, fellow human beings like myself." I wanted somehow to create a new path, to transform mistrust into trust, fear into confidence, an unhealthy lingering over the past into a commitment to the future. In every country I have visited, I have always felt how earnestly people everywhere yearn for peace.

The first condition for world peace is for people to really learn about each other, to start to really understand and appreciate each other. The surest way of melting the 'ice' of mistrust is to promote interaction among ordinary people — through meetings, visits, and cultural and educational exchange. Young people who are not caught up in the past can often lead the way.

Many years ago, it was the tradition among the Canadian Indian indigenous people to hold great celebrations when a daughter came of age.

Two daughters of a great chief had reached adulthood and a feast was being prepared. But news arrived that enemies to the north were preparing for war. The daughters went to their father and said, "Dear father! Someday we will become mothers and will give birth to children who will grow up to be strong chiefs like you. For their sake, please invite the people of the north to our celebration."

The chief could not refuse his daughters, so reluctantly he sent a message to his long-time enemies and invited them.

They came in great numbers, bringing their wives and children and many gifts. War songs changed into songs of joy.

Later the two sisters each gave birth to a son, and they became chiefs called Peace and Brotherly Love. Near Vancouver there is a beautiful twin-peaked mountain and according to legend, the two girls who loved peace became these peaks and still watch over Vancouver today.

The heart of even one peace-loving woman is strong; it can change society and reshape history.

I believe it is far too risky to leave the world's future in the hands of politicians. People must be wise and take action themselves to create peace. We must unite across borders: unite in our rejection of the idea of war itself. When the people of one country communicate with those of others, they can create a current towards peace. It is vital to create a network of people that transcends national borders so that a small number of corrupt leaders cannot break the webs of friendship and solidarity that join us.

Peace can never be attained by passively waiting for it. It is necessary for each of us, no matter how weak we feel we are, to build deep within our hearts a stronghold for peace that can withstand, and in the end silence, the incessant calls to war.

As Chilean poet Gabriela Mistral has written, "Have courage, my friends! For pacifism is not a sweet jam as some may think … Continue speaking out for peace, against the wind and the waves … Pacifism is not something easy. One must not abide injustice in silence. My friends, continue to cry out, until the circle of peace is expanded."

Real peace is only to be found in the realities of daily life. We must plant the seeds of a fundamental peace in the daily life of individuals, in our hearts and inner lives. And, we must protect and foster these seeds until they grow into the firm reality of peace for all.

Thus, it is up to us to construct a world without war. Whether we give up on this as an impossible goal, or whether we continue the challenge, however great the difficulties involved — on this the fate of the entire twenty-first century depends.